Off the Waitlist

A Practical Strategy for Canadians Who Can't
Afford to Wait

Ingrid Gahsner

Canada

IMI Canada

ISBN 978-1-0697740-0-2 (Paperback)

ISBN 978-1-0697740-1-9 (eBook)

Published by IMI Canada
Printed by Amazon / Available worldwide via Kindle Direct Publishing

Book Cover by Yuanni Liang

1st Edition, 2025

Acknowledgements

Thank you to my clients, whose stories and challenges inspired this book. Your willingness to share your frustration, your confusion, and your questions makes it clear that something has to change.

To the colleagues who supported this project from the very beginning — your encouragement, insight, and belief in the value of this work helped bring it to life.

A special thank you to Dr. Raymond Rupert, who generously took the time to review the earliest version of this manuscript. Your thoughtful feedback and professional insight gave me the clarity and confidence to keep going.

And finally, to Isaac and Marcelle — thank you for your patience, perspective, and for always reminding me what matters most.

Contents

Foreword

Raymond Rupert, MD, MBA

CEO, Healtheon & RCM Health Consultancy

I've had the privilege of assisting thousands of Canadians and their families throughout my 40-year career in family medicine, and later through my leadership at RCM Health and Healtheon. My work is grounded in a single mission: to ensure every patient receives timely, high-quality care — despite the system-wide barriers that often stand in the way.

One of the most powerful lessons in Ingrid Gahsner's *Off the Waitlist* mirrors a lesson I learned personally: that knowledge, courage, and persistence are often the only way to access proper care. When my daughter was diagnosed with sepsis, it was only through intense advocacy that we secured the urgent treatment she needed — and it saved her life.

As CEO of Healtheon and RCM Health Consultancy, I've seen the limitations of the public system up close: multi-year waits for specialists, administrative bottlenecks, and patients caught in an endless loop of referrals and delays. I've also seen how thoughtfully integrated private medical services — when used ethically and strategically — can lead to better outcomes, without undermining universal principles.

Ingrid's work as a Certified Healthcare Access Planner™ is revolutionary in that regard. She doesn't just offer insurance — she teaches people how to build access. Her guidance blends private, hybrid, and publicly funded channels into smart, personalized strategies that get patients the care they need, when they need it. This book shines a light on options too many Canadians don't even know exist — and, more importantly, shows us how to access them.

Off the Waitlist arrives at exactly the right moment. It's not enough to simply fund healthcare — we must empower people to advocate, navigate, and protect their own access in a system that often fails to deliver.

I endorse this book wholeheartedly. If you've ever felt frustrated, helpless, or confused by our healthcare system — whether for yourself, your children, or aging parents — this is the guide you've been waiting for. It's more than information. It's a roadmap to reclaiming control of your health, your time, and your outcomes.

Raymond Rupert, MD, MBA

CEO, Healtheon & RCM Health Consultancy

Introduction

If you've picked up this book, chances are you've run out of patience with the Canadian healthcare system. Or maybe you're simply curious — looking for answers, wondering what's going on, and when things might finally start to improve. Whatever the case, you're in the right place. This book speaks to both perspectives.

Personally, I lean more toward the first category. Yes, I want answers, and I hope for improvements — but that's secondary to my frustration with the delays. Like many others, I juggle multiple responsibilities every day. I'm a parent, a caregiver, a consultant. I'm the person others rely on to get things done. So, for me, long wait times aren't just inconvenient — they're unacceptable. As a Canadian, I honestly just expect more. I remember when wait times were reasonable, and that's still my point of reference.

That's why the current state of healthcare in Canada is so deeply concerning. Wait times now stretch from weeks to months. Referrals are delayed. Imaging is deferred. Surgeries are postponed — often multiple times. And when something urgent happens we find ourselves stuck in a system we can't influence — no matter how critical — with no real alternatives. The unavailability is staggering, and it's simply no longer tolerable.

Although it may appear otherwise, this book is not a critique of the public healthcare system — nor is it a political position. It's simply a straightforward, common sense analysis of what's really happening, where the system falls short, and how, with professional well informed guidance, you can plan around those limitations. No loopholes. No rule bending. Just real information, transparent costs, and modern planning strategies that put you back in control.

But this book isn't just informative — it introduces a new approach: one that treats healthcare access as a risk in its own right, demanding deliberate, forward thinking planning.

Because the truth is, we do have other options. Proven, accessible, and fully legal options that most Canadians have never heard of — not because they're hidden, but because paradigm shifts take time to gain traction. And right now, most Canadians haven't made that shift. Just like we plan for investments, retirement, education, or succession, the reality is that healthcare access must now be approached with the same level of intention. It's the only way to achieve timely medical care with any certainty of success.

If you haven't considered this before, that's completely understandable — this is a new way of thinking. It calls for a collective shift from passive reliance to proactive personal responsibility. And while it may be hard to admit, this is a reality we can no longer afford to ignore: universal healthcare, in its current form, is no longer sufficient to meet the needs of Canadians.

Waiting and hoping is no longer a strategy. Planning is.

Maybe one day the system will improve — and we can all hope that it does. But hope doesn't help when you're facing a waitlist for critical surgery or a delayed diagnosis. Canadians need to know what they can do now. This book offers solutions for the present, because your health — and the health of those who depend on you — can't always wait for long term change.

This perspective doesn't offer promises. It lays out the reality — and then gives you a clear, actionable strategy to regain control, protect the people who depend on you, and eliminate the guesswork from one of the most vital aspects of your life: access to medical care.

This isn't about theory, politics, or persuasion. It's about structure, practicality, and having a plan.

Welcome to a new way of thinking about healthcare in Canada.

Let's begin.

Ingrid Gahsner

Chapter 1

When Coverage Isn't Enough

As Canadians, most of us assume our health is protected by universal healthcare — our beloved, free, accessible, equitable public system. It's a source of national pride and a defining part of our identity. We've come to expect it will be there for us, no matter what. Whether the issue is big or small, urgent or routine, we trust that we'll be covered. No cost. No strings. No hassle. No worry.

But what happens when that system is stretched too thin? When the care you need is available — but inaccessible at the same time? When appointments are booked months in advance, imaging is backlogged, referrals stall in endless loops, or surgeries are postponed — not once, but again and again? What happens when the very system you've trusted to protect you becomes the reason you're stuck waiting?

You may still be covered. But without access, are you truly protected?

This chapter is about that distinction — the gap between what we believe we're protected against and what actually happens when illness or injury meets the limits of our healthcare system. It's about the difference between being covered in theory and supported in reality.

In addition, it's about what it costs to wait — physically, financially, emotionally, and functionally — making it clear that access to timely medical care is more important than you think. Because this isn't just a theoretical gap, it's the Canadian reality.

Let me show you what it looks like in practice.

Case Study: When the System Runs Out of Time – Alex's Story

Alex was 52 — a founder, a father, a cyclist. He was the kind of person who always had a plan: for his business, his finances, and his family. When he began losing strength in his right hand, he immediately made an appointment with his family doctor. She suspected something neurological and referred him for an MRI, but the wait time was eight weeks.

By the time the scan was completed and reviewed, the diagnosis was clear: glioblastoma. It was advanced and aggressive, and treatment began too late. Alex didn't lack discipline, health awareness, or insurance — he lacked time. And the system couldn't give it to him.

His story isn't rare. It isn't the result of bad luck or poor choices, but of a system that simply couldn't move fast enough — not because it didn't care, but because it wasn't designed to.

And he's not alone.

Medical Risk: When The Delay Is Deadlier Than the Diagnosis

Alex's story shows the truth most Canadians don't realize until it's too late: in today's healthcare environment, the biggest threat isn't just the illness — it's the delay. When something goes wrong physically, you don't just need a diagnosis — you need one fast. You don't just need treatment — you need the right treatment, at the right moment. The sooner you move, the more options you have. The longer it takes, the fewer remain. And while this example involved glioblastoma — an aggressive cancer — this risk extends far beyond any one condition.

No matter what the illness, when access to care is delayed, there is always the possibility of progression to a more urgent, even untreatable stage. Cancer metastasizes. Heart disease silently worsens. Autoimmune conditions quietly damage nerves and organs. Like Alex, in many cases, the treatment window closes before the patient even knows what's wrong.

Surgeries, too, can come with consequences when delayed. A herniated disc can turn into nerve damage. A minor joint issue may evolve into permanent mobility loss. What could have been a straightforward procedure becomes more invasive — or impossible. Even time sensitive emergencies can be missed entirely. Delayed diagnoses for strokes, aneurysms, or retinal detachment don't just increase the risk — they often determine whether a person lives or dies, recovers or becomes permanently disabled.

And for those with complex or rare conditions, the lack of access to specialists and advanced testing can lead to years of misdiagnosis, or no diagnosis at all. Without the right input at the right time, the risk of deterioration increases — one system at a time. As conditions compound, one untreated issue cascades into another. Cardiac delays contribute to kidney strain. Inflammatory diseases cause multi-organ inflammation. Infections spread. Tumors grow. Over time, untreated conditions don't just persist — they can transform into more advanced, resistant, or complicated forms that are far harder to treat effectively.

From a medical perspective, this is what delay risk looks like in real life. It's not theoretical. It's clinical. And it's dangerous. Because even if you have a trusted family doctor, a hospital nearby, or even a cousin who's a cardiac surgeon, if you can't get in front of the right person, access the right diagnostics, or schedule the right treatment soon enough — then you're not protected. You're exposed.

The danger doesn't end with your health. What begins as a medical delay can quickly spiral into a financial crisis — especially when timely care isn't accessible through the public system.

Financial Risks: The High Cost of Delay

Healthcare delays don't just threaten your physical well-being, they put your financial security at risk.

When timely public care isn't available, many Canadians are left with no choice but to seek alternatives. Some turn to private options within Canada; others travel abroad for surgery, diagnostics, or experimental treatments. But wherever you go, one thing is consistent: the cost is out-of-pocket — and it can be substantial, often reaching tens or even hundreds of thousands of dollars.

The real risk lies in how unplanned these expenses are. Most people don't anticipate them, especially not at the exact moment when care is urgently needed. This leads to reactive decisions — accepting whatever option is available, often at a premium, because there's no time to compare or strategize.

Private care, for Canadians, is never reimbursed by traditional insurance, so these aren't just unexpected costs — they're uninsured costs. And the urgency of the situation accelerates wealth depletion. Large, unplanned withdrawals from savings, investments, or credit can erase years of financial planning in just a few months.

And it doesn't stop with your bank account. The stress of navigating delays — especially when time, money, and health are on the line — takes a serious emotional toll.

Emotional and Psychological Risks: The Mental Toll of Waiting

The emotional burden of waiting can be just as disruptive as the medical condition itself.

Living in chronic uncertainty while symptoms worsen — with no diagnosis, no timeline, and no plan — leads to anxiety, emotional exhaustion, and even breakdown. Many people describe feeling forgotten, dismissed, or stuck in a loop where the only option is to wait and worry.

This emotional strain is particularly acute for those who rely on clarity and stability to lead teams or take care of others. The fear of losing health, identity, or control becomes overwhelming — and often shows up in disrupted sleep, reduced productivity, strained relationships, and an inability to focus.

Even beyond fear, isolation sets in. Being unwell without a clear explanation — and with no roadmap for what comes next — is a deeply lonely experience. The healthcare system's silence becomes a stressor in itself.

And over time, that silence becomes more than emotional — it becomes disruptive. Because when answers are delayed and care is out of reach, it's not just your mindset that suffers. It's your entire life.

Functional Risks: When Life Falls Out of Rhythm

When timely care isn't available, the disruption doesn't stop at your health. It interrupts every aspect of your day to day routine — your ability to function, to fulfill obligations, and to maintain a sense of normalcy.

Without proper treatment, your condition can deteriorate to the point where basic routines are no longer manageable. You may find yourself needing help with everyday tasks, losing independence, or being forced to step back from responsibilities you once handled with ease.

Caregiver burden increases as well. When medical needs go unmet, family members often step in to fill the gaps — rearranging schedules, taking time off work, or managing complex care needs at home. This adds strain not just to you, but to your entire support network.

And for those in their prime working years, the cost is steep. Delays can sideline a career, put a business on hold, or force early retirement. What starts as a health delay can quickly become a disruption in productivity, income, and long-term financial stability.

Taken together, these risks paint a clear picture: healthcare delays are not just inconvenient — they are consequential. Medically, financially, emotionally, and functionally, the fallout can be devastating. This isn't a hypothetical risk. It's a real and growing threat — one that should be taken seriously by anyone who values their health, their wealth, or their ability to lead a full life.

And yet, many Canadians — even those who understand the severity of wait times — continue to act as if the system will come through when it matters most. They assume things will improve, that they'll stay healthy, or that their past good fortune will carry them forward. Some believe they're immune because they feel fine today. Others assume they'll age like their parents — quietly and without complication.

But none of those beliefs change the reality: the risk isn't down the road — it's here, right now. And if your only plan is to hope the system holds up, then you don't have a plan at all, because hope is not a strategy.

When the System Fails, What's Your Backup?

Hope is a powerful thing. It lifts us in dark moments, helps us endure uncertainty, and gives us something to hold onto when outcomes are beyond our control. But when it comes to your health — especially within a system defined by delays and unpredictability — hope alone isn't enough. It won't get you an earlier appointment, a faster diagnosis, or timely treatment. In those moments, what you need is a plan.

Hope waits. Strategy prepares. Hope assumes the system will eventually come through. Strategy asks, *what if it doesn't?*

That shift — from passive belief to active preparation — is the foundation of everything in this book. It's the difference between blind faith and deliberate action. Between reacting to problems and anticipating them. Between feeling powerless and being in control.

This isn't just a mindset shift. It's a structural one. It means thinking differently about timelines, access, and readiness — and building a plan that accounts for alternative care options, availability, and cost before the crisis hits. It's the same logic you use with every other risk. You don't buy car insurance after an accident, invest in a pension plan after you've retired, or buy life insurance after your dead.

So why would you leave your healthcare to chance?

You don't rely on hope to protect your income, your assets, or your future — so it's time to stop relying on it to protect you from medical delays. And to be clear, this isn't about abandoning the public system. It's about acknowledging its limits — and filling the gaps with intention, foresight, and professional guidance.

Navigating the System

The risks outlined in this chapter aren't theoretical — they're real, immediate, and already affecting thousands of Canadians at every stage of life. And while patriotic belief in the system may offer comfort, it's no substitute for timely access to care.

The only rational response is planning. Because when the system falters — and increasingly, it does — the only thing that separates those who move forward from those who fall behind is preparation. It's the most reliable way to protect yourself from the unexpected.

And to be clear, planning doesn't mean abandoning the public system. It means acknowledging that it's no longer the comprehensive solution it once was — and recognizing that a time may come when you'll need something more. It also means learning how to navigate what's available and what isn't — using the public system for what it does well, while identifying alternate options for what it can't deliver in time.

Strategic planning isn't a rejection of the system — it's a way to work within it, without being limited by it.

In the next chapter, we'll take a closer look at health-care planning — beginning with the traditional strategies Canadians have relied on for decades. But those solutions weren't designed for the access challenges we face today.

Delayed care has introduced a new kind of risk — one that fundamentally changes how protection must be approached. Responding to this isn't just about refining old ideas — it's about building a new modern strategy from the ground up.

One where access risk becomes the foundation, not the afterthought.

Chapter 2

Why Traditional Planning Falls Short

In the last chapter, we uncovered a difficult truth: having provincial coverage isn't the same as being protected — and because delayed care can be so detrimental, lack of access must now be considered a critical risk factor. That realization laid the foundation for a new mindset — one that replaces reliance with readiness and reframes health-care access planning as essential, not optional.

But a mindset shift alone isn't enough — it must be followed by a structural shift in planning that accounts for this new kind of risk. It requires a new perspective, and that's what this book is here to offer: a modern lens on healthcare planning that redefines the strategy from the ground up.

The core problem is this: traditional solutions have never accounted for access risk. Not because it was ignored —

but because it didn't exist. The systems, products and assumptions we've long relied on were built for a different time. A time when care was easily accessible, when exposure was only financial, and when protection was defined by coverage alone.

In this chapter, we'll break down what traditional healthcare planning looks like — product by product — and examine what each one offers, and where it falls short when it comes to planning for access. We'll explore the structure, the fine print, and walk through real world case studies that highlight the blind spots. Because if you're relying on these products as your Plan B, those gaps could leave you unexpectedly exposed.

An Overview of the Basics

A traditional healthcare plan typically includes three insured products layered on top of the public system: disability insurance, critical illness insurance, and extended health benefits. There are many ways to structure these, and while we won't go into technical detail here, they've long been considered the foundational tools of personal healthcare planning in Canada.

Each of these products emerged in response to the gaps left by public healthcare, beginning with the rise of employer sponsored benefit plans in 1960, disability insurance in

1980, and critical illness a decade later. Since then, these tools have formed the gold standard in traditional health-care planning. They've been trusted by employers, re-lied on by professionals, and widely accepted as sufficient. Though separate in function, they all share a common design assumption: that the public system would deliver timely foundational care.

But from a modern access perspective, none of these prod-ucts delivers the right protection. They don't guarantee faster care, secure a diagnosis, or move you to the front of the line. They serve a purpose — and often a valuable one — but they weren't built to address the access crisis Canadians face today.

Let's move on to examine each in greater detail.

What Is Disability Insurance?

If you need to take time off work due to illness or injury, this coverage provides you with monthly payments that replace your salary from your employer. It's often the first layer of financial defense in a long-term health disrup-tion – and to be fair, it's a smart step – even though you can't get full protection. Under CRA regulations, even the most comprehensive individual disability policies can replace only up to 66.67% of your pre-disability income from a single source.

Disability coverage typically falls into two categories: short-term disability, which provides income from the first day you're off work for up to six months, and long-term disability, which continues that protection beyond the short-term window — often for periods of five years or until age 65.

These coverages can be purchased individually, included in an employer-sponsored benefits plan, or structured as a standalone corporate wage loss replacement plan. The rules around benefit limits and eligibility vary depending on how the plan is set up, as is the taxation of the income.

All disability policies are income based and, outside of the group plan scenario, they require income verification through tax returns to determine the maximum amount you can receive. Individual policies are medically under-written, which means good health is required to qualify, but they offer more flexibility and customization. Group policies are generally non-medical and easier to obtain but come with more restrictions and are tied to your employ-ment status.

While there are other technical differences between policy types, this summary should provide a general overview of how disability insurance functions.

Where it Falls Short

If you ever become ill or suffer an injury and your condition qualifies as a total disability, this insurance will kick in to assist with expenses. But it's important to understand that, even if you have both short-term and long-term protection, you could still go months without receiving a payment because claims typically take 30 to 60 days to process - and that's assuming your claim is approved without delay.

Now looking at this product from the perspective of your healthcare plan, you can see that if you're relying on income replacement alone as your Plan B, it falls short in many areas. In fact, you may find yourself in a worst case scenario, out of action, operating on a reduced salary (or no salary), while stuck in the public system waiting for care.

And without any other proactive strategy in place, that means one thing: you're waiting, in pain, stressed, anxious, and burning time you can't afford to lose.

This reality becomes even more precarious for self-employed professionals, consultants, contractors, and business owners. Many don't qualify for individual disability coverage because their reported income is too low to justify the purchase, and they often lack access to group plans due to minimum employee requirements. As a result, many choose to go without coverage altogether. In this case, their situation is even worse as they have no income replacement whatsoever to cover downtime.

Then there's the higher income professional who has a group plan but still isn't adequately protected. Why? Because most group disability policies cap the maximum benefit. So, while the plan may promise to cover 66.67% of your income, the actual payout might be limited to $3,000 or $5,000 a month – which may end up being 50% or less of your actual take home pay.

The Income Gap No One Talks About

This gap is something that rarely gets explained. Most people don't realize they're underinsured until they're already off work and doing the math, which, by then, is too late.

In reality, the ideal structure for a higher income earner with group plan coverage includes, a) the plan for basic coverage and, b) a personalized individual policy to top-up what you get at work. One without the other leaves exposure. But because most employers are focused on providing benefits within a budget, only one side of the equation is usually addressed. The full strategy never gets built.

So, what does that mean?

It means that income protection, while essential, is just one piece of a much larger puzzle. And when it's not integrated into a broader healthcare access strategy, it creates a dangerous illusion of security.

The Fine Print That Can Deny Your Claim

If you're relying on disability insurance to protect your income during a health crisis, it's critical to understand what the policy actually covers, and what it doesn't.

Disability insurance only pays out if you meet the policy's definition of total disability. In most cases, this means being unable to perform the substantial duties of your own occupation. It sounds straightforward - until you try to make a claim. To qualify for benefits, you must be deemed unable to work based on your physician's report and the conditions outlined in your policy. If those criteria aren't met, no benefit is payable.

And yes - for the advisors reading this - I'm simplifying. We can enhance professional policies with riders and additional protections, but no matter how comprehensive the plan, the core definition of total disability must still be satisfied before anything else applies.

You may be in pain. You may be undergoing tests. You may be completely unable to function at your normal level. But unless your condition meets the insurer's definition of total disability, your claim can be denied or delayed.

Partial disabilities - where you're technically able to perform some work - often don't qualify for benefits, depending on the type of policy you've purchased. Intermittent or hard-to-diagnose conditions can also be even more difficult to claim.

And even if your claim is approved, the benefit will only replace a portion of your income — and it may be taxable. To continue receiving payments, you'll typically need to provide ongoing proof that you remain totally disabled as defined by the policy. In many cases, the insurance company will also require your file to be reviewed by an appointed physician to determine continued eligibility.

Case Study: Falling Through the Cracks of Coverage

Take Jason, a 48-year-old corporate lawyer who developed severe nerve pain in his right arm. Something to do with the disk in his neck. It wasn't a clear-cut diagnosis, just ongoing discomfort that made it unbearable to use his arm. His lifestyle was completely disrupted and his ability to work compromised.

He wasn't completely disabled. He could still show up to work, technically. But his output dropped. He couldn't meet deadlines. He was making mistakes. And the stress of being barely functional, without any real diagnosis or treatment option, made things worse.

When he filed a claim through his short-term disability policy, it was denied. The insurer's rationale? He wasn't totally disabled under the policy definition, there was no clear diagnosis, and he could still perform some of the duties of his job despite the enhanced occupation coverage that was added to his base policy. Still, no payout.

Jason was left working at half mass, with less income, no medical care, and no answers.

Frustrated and exhausted, he found himself in a mental fog - physically impaired, financially strained, and emotionally isolated, with no clear path forward

Why Disability Insurance Alone Isn't Enough

Here's the problem with relying solely on disability insurance. First, payouts are conditional — you must meet strict definitions of total disability to qualify. Second, the benefit often falls short, typically replacing only a portion of your income — and sometimes far less than you actually earn. Third, you may not qualify at all because pre-existing conditions, insufficient income, or other disqualifiers can block access.

And most importantly, through the lens of modern planning, income protection is not the same as access to care. Disability insurance won't move you up a surgical waitlist, get you a faster appointment with a specialist, or fund international treatment if you want to skip the line.

Let's revisit the real-world example above. Jason didn't just need time off or income replacement. He needed a diagnosis - and fast. He needed access to timely, expert care so he could figure out what was wrong, begin treatment and return to work with as little disruption as possible. In his case, a disability payout up to $2000 / week of his income - even if approved - wasn't the solution. What he needed was a plan that bypassed bottlenecks and bought him time, clarity, and results.

Disability insurance is a valuable tool. It belongs in every well-rounded financial plan. But by itself, it's not enough. In fact, in many situations, it's not even close. It's a safety net - not a roadmap.

While this policy offers conditional income protection, many turn to critical illness insurance for lump-sum support during a major diagnosis. This coverage is easier to get, but like disability it also comes with significant blind spots that are often misunderstood.

What is Critical Illness Insurance?

Critical illness insurance is often seen as a smart addition to a healthcare protection strategy — a way to cushion the financial blow of a serious diagnosis. But while its purpose is clear, the way it functions is often misunderstood. Many people assume that having a policy in place means they're fully protected, when in reality, the structure of the coverage comes with important limitations that can impact whether — and when — it pays out.

At its core, a critical illness policy provides a lump-sum payout if you're diagnosed with one of the covered conditions. Depending on the policy, that list can range from as few as four conditions to more than two dozen, typically including cancer, heart attack, stroke, multiple sclerosis, and others.

Like disability policies, this coverage can be purchased individually, through an employee benefits plan, or structured under a corporate group policy. Policies are medically underwritten but maximum amounts aren't established based on income.

Where It Falls Short

While critical illness insurance can be a valuable financial tool, it's important to understand when you're not protected.

Injuries Aren't Covered: CI policies are designed to cover specific illnesses - not accidents. So, if you fall, suffer a head injury, and develop ongoing migraines that force you off work, you won't qualify for a payout.

Survival Requirement: Most policies include a 30-day survival clause. If you're diagnosed with a serious condition, like a heart issue requiring urgent surgery, but pass away within 30 days, no benefit will be paid, even if the condition itself was covered.

Initial Waiting Period: Policies often include a 90-day exclusion period from the start date. If you're diagnosed with a critical illness during this time, your claim won't be eligible for payment.

Strict Definitions Apply: Covered illnesses must meet specific, often technical, definitions. For example, a breast cancer diagnosis must be classified as invasive or life-threatening to trigger a payout. Early-stage or non-invasive forms (like DCIS) typically don't qualify unless additional coverage was added.

Why Critical Illness Alone Isn't Enough

Given its limitations, it becomes clear why critical illness insurance alone isn't sufficient as your Plan B. That's not to say it doesn't hold value - it absolutely does. But much like disability insurance, CI is just one piece of a much larger puzzle. On its own, it doesn't function as a comprehensive healthcare access strategy.

Also, the core issue remains the same. Critical illness doesn't give you faster access to care. Unless it's been intentionally integrated into a broader, proactive plan, it won't help you skip the waitlist or navigate treatment options more efficiently.

Revisiting our earlier example with Jason - his symptoms may not result in a diagnosis that qualifies for a critical illness payout. And without a confirmed, covered condition, the policy provides no support. It won't expedite diagnostics, secure specialist consultations, or help him access treatment more quickly.

Now, to the advisors reading this, you might be nodding in agreement but also thinking: if Jason's condition had been covered, then the payout could help him access care privately. And you're right - but only to a point.

Let's consider another example.

Case Study: The Gap Between Funding and Access

Priya is diagnosed with leukemia. Her CI policy includes no waiting period beyond the standard 30-day survival clause. Her claim is approved, and within days, she receives a $150,000 tax-free lump sum. That's a powerful benefit. But she quickly learns that the waitlist for stem cell therapy in Canada is long, and she may not even qualify due to eligibility restrictions. She decides to pursue treatment abroad, using her CI payout to fund it.

But emotionally, she's overwhelmed - grappling not only with a life-altering diagnosis, but also the sudden burden of navigating complex decisions around international care, alone and under pressure.

Here's the challenge: Priya never planned to use her benefit this way, and she has no idea how much private treatment will actually cost, where to go for advanced or specialized care, or how to access that care quickly, safely, and reliably.

And Priya's situation isn't unique. Most people assume the public system will be there when they need it - and that a CI payout of $100,000 or even $250,000 will be enough. But depending on the diagnosis and the treatment location, that amount can fall far short. In Priya's case, just one round of stem cell therapy in Germany currently exceeds €380,000.

So yes, a critical illness policy can be valuable — if it pays out. But even then, it doesn't come with a support structure. And when paired with disability insurance, these products still fall short of addressing the logistical and emotional challenges involved in accessing care. They don't help you identify top private clinics, evaluate international treatment options, book diagnostics or surgery faster, coordinate post-operative care or recovery abroad, or navigate the complex journey of cross-border medical care.

You may have some money - but you're still on your own. It's like being handed a map without a guide, and realizing it's upside down. And more often than not anyone with CI in their portfolio right now hasn't consider any of this – so in reality, they probably still don't have enough money.

Now let's look at the final piece of the traditional puzzle – the supplemental health and dental plan. Great product. But it also comes with limitations of its own.

What Are Group Benefit Plans?

Provided by employers, these plans are set up through private businesses. They have been the cornerstone of healthcare planning in Canada for decades, designed to supplement the public system by providing products and services that the province doesn't cover.

If you're employed by a company with coverage, or you've created a plan for your own team as a business owner, you likely have access to coverage for prescriptions, medical services and equipment, vision, travel, dental, and professional services. And, as mentioned above, some plans also include basic disability and critical illness insurance.

Where They Fall Short

First and foremost, it's important to understand that employer sponsored benefit plans are entirely optional. Unlike other systems where certain coverage is mandated, employers in Canada are under no obligation to offer these plans. As a result, many individuals have no workplace coverage at all.

For those who do, the scope and quality of coverage can vary significantly. The landscape is inconsistent and often unpredictable. Employers have full discretion to introduce, modify, or even cancel a benefits plan - frequently without employee consultation or notice.

If you're counting on these benefits as your Plan B, you may one day find that key elements of your coverage have changed, or that reimbursement limits have been quietly reduced - leaving you unexpectedly vulnerable.

In the next section, we'll take a closer look at one of the most critical components of these plans and how its limitations can directly impact your access to care.

The Hidden Limits of Drug Coverage

Drug coverage is one of the most misunderstood components of group benefit plans. Many Canadians assume that if they have coverage through work, their prescriptions will be fully covered - no questions asked. But that assumption can be dangerously misleading.

Prescription medications are among the most expensive and emotionally charged aspects of healthcare. And while group plans can help, their support is limited, conditional, and often subject to change without warning.

One of the most overlooked limitations? Annual drug caps. Most group drug plans come with a maximum reimbursement amount, ranging anywhere from $1,500 to unlimited per person per year - with $3,000 being the most common ceiling. That may sound reasonable - until you or a family member needs a specialty drug, biologic, or advanced therapy.

Many of today's life-changing medications cost well over $1,000 a month. Some exceed $10,000 annually. Once you hit your plan's cap, every dollar beyond that is out of pocket.

Why Don't Employers Increase the Drug Limits?

Because raising drug caps - especially to unlimited maximums - can have major financial consequences. Employers are often advised against it, since doing so triggers the need for reinsurance (a costly backup policy designed to protect against extreme claims). If even one employee has over $10,000 in annual drug costs, the employer becomes what the industry calls unmarketable - meaning their group plan becomes harder, or even impossible, to shop competitively in future renewals.

And even moderate increases come at a cost. For example, a $5,000 drug cap gives employees more spending power - but that also means higher total claims and a spike in premiums. To keep costs predictable and maintain plan flexibility, most employers choose to cap drug coverage conservatively. Understandable from a budgeting stand-point - but it leaves employees exposed, especially as med-ication needs increase due to age, chronic illness, or serious diagnosis.

And that's just one piece of the problem. Even if a drug is listed on your plan, it often requires prior authoriza-tion - a bureaucratic process involving paperwork, delays, and potential denials. Expensive medications frequently require approval - and are sometimes rejected outright. And if a drug hasn't been approved by Health Canada - even if it's widely used or considered the gold standard internationally - your group plan won't cover it at all.

The bottom line? Your benefits plan may look solid on paper, but when it comes to serious or ongoing medica-tion needs, its support is often limited, unpredictable, and reactive. Group drug coverage isn't a strategy, it's a stopgap - and one with a ceiling.

Why Group Plans ≠ Strategy

And back to the core issue: like disability and critical illness insurance, a supplemental benefit plan can't shield you from delays in the healthcare system. It's a valuable product and certainly has a place within a broader strategy - but on its own, it doesn't constitute a comprehensive healthcare plan.

These plans help with medications and some care related costs, but they don't offer access. They won't move you up a waitlist. They won't connect you with specialists. And they won't coordinate private care when timing is critical. So, if you've been thinking of your benefits plan as your healthcare safety net, it's time to reconsider. It's coverage - not a strategy.

Rethinking the Foundation

After reviewing the traditional products, it should now be clear why this deeper examination matters. Here's the reality when viewed through the lens of access risk.

What good is a $250,000 critical illness policy to a client who needs to fly to Austria for hernia surgery just to avoid a year long wait in Canada? Or a long-term disability plan for someone with nerve damage who can't see a neurologist for 12 months? Or a drug benefit with a $5,000 annual cap when the medication they need isn't even available in the country?

We keep returning to the same core message: having coverage is no longer the same as being protected. These products have value — but in this context they can't function as your Plan B. And the products themselves are only half the problem. The broader issue now is that healthcare planning as a discipline is outdated. Access risk is such a new concept that most insurance and financial professionals — the very people responsible for building these plans — are still in the dark.

That's why it's time to evolve.

A mindset shift alone isn't enough — it must be followed by a structural shift in planning.

That change requires a modern understanding of the healthcare system, awareness of where delays occur, the alternative options available, and the ability to build strategies that go beyond payouts and reimbursement. It means repositioning traditional products within a broader, integrated plan — one that includes solutions designed specifically to address access risk.

Because today, having coverage is no longer the same as having access — or control. And good planning is the only way to reclaim both.

What You Need to Know Moving Forward

You may already have some — or all — of the products we reviewed in this chapter. If so, the goal wasn't to discredit them, but to give you a clearer understanding of how they actually function, so you can better evaluate their role in your personal healthcare plan. As we move forward, we'll explain how a modern access plan is built — but before that, it's essential to understand the healthcare landscape itself, both public and private. Because in Canada, comprehensive planning now requires multiple layers.

We began with traditional products — their strengths, limitations, and the planning assumptions they were built on. But those limitations wouldn't be nearly as dangerous if the public system could reliably fill the gaps. As you'll see in the next chapter, it can't — and, in fact, it was never built to. Rather than acting as a safety net, the system has become one of the greatest barriers to timely, effective care.

In Chapter 3, we'll pull back the curtain on what's really standing between you and the public care you need — the legislative restrictions, the resource illusions, and the cultural beliefs that keep reform stalled and patients stuck. Because before you can plan around the system, you need to understand why it works the way it does — and who it's actually built to serve.

Chapter 3

What's Really Blocking Your Care

For more than a decade, healthcare delays have steadily worsened — but even as frustration mounts, Canadians continue to defend the system. We've been conditioned to believe that long waits are the price we pay for fairness, and that eventually, with enough time and funding, the system will fix itself. But that narrative is starting to crack — because lived experience tells a different story. The delays are no longer tolerable. The gaps are no longer hidden. And the consequences? They're real, measurable, and increasingly impossible to ignore.

This chapter isn't about policy for its own sake.

It's about understanding the deeper forces behind the breakdown in access — the structural, political, and ideological barriers that shape your experience of care. Because if you're going to build a modern healthcare strategy, you need to stop relying on outdated assumptions and start facing what's actually in the way.

To understand what's really blocking your access, we need to go beyond headlines and dig into the design itself — starting with how the system was built to control care, not deliver it efficiently.

Structural Barriers: The Design That Delays

In Canada's single payer model, provincial governments control the funding for medically necessary services. Because healthcare is one of the largest budgetary expenses, controlling access to these services becomes a tool for controlling cost. That control is exercised by capping what gets funded — whether it's operating room hours, imaging slots, diagnostic tests, or physician billings. The result is a system that slows the flow of care intentionally.

Hospitals can't run at full capacity without additional funding — even if they have the space, staff, or willingness. A fully equipped operating room may sit idle because the budget only allows it to run three days a week. A surgeon ready to work may be limited by quotas. An MRI machine may be available, but not approved for weekend operation due to union constraints, staffing shortages, or rigid budget cycles. Even family physicians face billing caps that restrict how many patients they can see — regardless of community demand. It's all dictated by the amount of money the province allocates to healthcare.

This built-in rationing isn't random — it's part of the design. The system was created to be publicly funded, but that funding is limited. So instead of being mobilized, medical resources are deliberately constrained to stay within these limits. Tied up in systems that prioritize process over people. That's why the infrastructure we do have — hospitals, clinics, specialists, and equipment — isn't being leveraged for performance. It's being managed for control.

On paper, the system looks solid. But dig even slightly beneath the surface, and a different picture emerges — one where resources are rationed, not maximized. Restricted, not scaled. Managed by policy — not by patient need.

You're not waiting because care doesn't exist. You're waiting because the rules say you must — regardless of your urgency, your condition, or your risk. And that's one of the most misunderstood — and most dangerous — aspects of the Canadian healthcare system. Access isn't about ability. It's about permission.

Until that changes, waiting will remain the default. Innovation will remain stalled. And timely, strategic care will remain out of reach. Not because we lack the means, but because we've boxed them in.

This isn't just a philosophical or policy problem — it plays out in real, practical ways every single day. The pieces are in place. But they're not being activated.

Here's what that looks like in real life.

Case Study: The Surgery That Couldn't Happen — Until It Did

James, a 58-year-old executive in Calgary, began experiencing worsening pain in his lower abdomen. After a visit to his family doctor and a series of inconclusive tests, a CT scan was recommended. But the public wait time was 11 weeks — just for the scan. The specialist consultation that followed would take another 6 months. James had the option to wait and hope it wasn't serious — or act.

He chose to act.

Through a private clinic, James paid $1,300 for a CT scan and saw a urologist within ten days. The diagnosis: a complex inguinal hernia requiring surgical repair. His surgeon, a senior specialist in the public system, agreed to perform the procedure — but James was told he'd be waiting up to a year for a date. Not because the surgeon wasn't available, but because the operating room itself wasn't.

The hospital's surgical schedule was maxed out. Staffing budgets were frozen. The operating room sat idle evenings and weekends, even as patients like James waited in pain.

Unable to put his life on hold — and unwilling to risk complications — James flew to Vancouver and paid out-of-pocket at a private surgical center that contracted the same specialist who worked in the public system in Calgary. The surgery was done in less than two weeks. Recovery was smooth. Life resumed.

What changed wasn't the diagnosis or the skill of the surgeon. It was access — to space, to time, to funding. Every element of care existed in Calgary. The system simply wouldn't allow it to happen there due to restrictions. So, James stepped outside of the system and was taken care of immediately.

Beds, scanners, and skilled professionals are often left underused — not because capacity is lacking, but because the system isn't built to mobilize them. Rigid budgets, outdated billing models, and policy constraints keep resources offline. The result? Bottlenecks created by structure, not by clinical need.

Behind this structure lies a legacy system built on cost containment and equity, not performance. The Canada Health Act was created to prevent financial barriers at the point of care — but it also unintentionally gave governments a strong incentive to limit how much care is actually delivered.

The result is a system that confuses fairness with sameness — where access is often determined not by urgency or outcome, but by how to ensure no one gets more than anyone else, even if everyone ends up with less. The problem isn't lack of care. It's lack of access to the care that already exists.

This is one of the most persistent myths in Canadian healthcare — the belief that our system is failing because we don't have enough resources. But the truth is, we don't lack the ability to deliver excellent care — we lack a system that allows it to function at the level it needs to. And that's no accident. The structural rigidity that holds it back isn't just inefficient. It's legislated.

Political Barriers: Laws, Silence and Stalemates

At the center of this dysfunction lies a deeper structural barrier: the Canada Health Act. Originally designed to ensure fairness and universal access, the Act has become a legal bottleneck — one that limits innovation, restricts alternatives, and blocks faster care, even when the capacity exists.

While this book doesn't dive into the full history of healthcare policy, there's one foundational truth you need to understand: the system you're relying on today is governed by legislation introduced in the 1950s and formalized in 1984 under the Canada Health Act.

At the time, the intent was clear — to guarantee access to publicly funded healthcare with no fees charged at the point of use. It was a value driven framework, rooted in equity and cost control. And for a long time it worked. The Act helped standardize care across provinces and protected Canadians from catastrophic out-of-pocket costs.

But here's what most people don't realize — and what matters most today: the Act doesn't just enable public care; it actively limits the development of private alternatives. And that's where the real problems begin. Because no matter which side of the debate you're on, this restriction doesn't just impact private options — it makes the public system worse.

When private alternatives are disallowed, everyone, regardless of risk or urgency, is forced to wait in the same overloaded queue. This traps pressure inside the public system instead of relieving it, ultimately worsening the wait for everyone.

In today's environment of chronic delays, specialist shortages, and extensive surgical waitlists, it's obvious the public system can't improve fast enough. But under the current legal framework, provinces risk losing federal health transfers if they allow private clinics to charge for medically necessary services.

So, in other words, by blocking the growth of a parallel system, we're stuck with no other options when the provinces won't invest more in healthcare. This was never the intention of the Act, but in practice, that's exactly what it does. While other countries use private options to relieve pressure on public infrastructure, in Canada, the law traps pressure inside it.

The result? Public care is overloaded and lacks capacity. Private care is restricted by regulation and funding threats.

And the Act hasn't been meaningfully updated in over 40 years — despite massive shifts in population, technology, and medical demand. The result is a rigid, risk-averse policy environment where any attempt to innovate feels like navigating a political minefield.

But this stagnation is no longer just a policy issue — it's a frontline reality. A growing number of physicians, healthcare professionals, and policy leaders are raising the same concern: the system wasn't built for modern complexity. It wasn't designed for speed, precision, or proactive care. And now, it's cracking under the pressure of needs it was never built to meet.

That's why understanding the legal limitations isn't just helpful — it's essential.

Because if you want faster access to care and better outcomes, your strategy must account for the rules that restrict innovation — and the workarounds that still exist within them. Otherwise, you're stuck relying on a system that was never built to move quickly and shows no sign of reform anytime soon.

But the obstacles to progress aren't just legal or structural — they're also emotional. Even if policy was modified to allow for change, cultural resistance can stop it in its tracks. And few topics trigger that resistance more strongly than the idea of profit in healthcare.

It's Easier to Avoid Than Explain

Let's be honest — the topic is complex. It doesn't fit neatly into a headline, and it certainly doesn't translate easily into political talking points. It requires nuance, education, and thoughtful communication.

That's hard to package. It's hard to campaign on. And it's even harder to lead with when your audience has been conditioned to fear it. Explaining that other countries offer both universal public care and private options — with better outcomes and shorter wait times — takes time and clarity. It means reframing decades of deeply held assumptions and challenging myths that have hardened into political absolutes.

For most policymakers, that kind of effort is simply too politically risky — so they avoid the topic altogether. Instead, they continue to campaign on promises of increased funding, even though they know it won't make a meaningful difference. Real change requires major reconstruction, not more money poured into a broken framework. Otherwise, you get more of the same.

It delays reform, blocks innovation, and leaves patients stuck in a system that no longer works the way it was intended to. Despite mounting evidence that the system is struggling — and waitlists growing longer each year — the conversation around reform remains paralyzed in government. Not by lack of data or viable solutions, but by something more powerful: the political risk of challenging the status quo.

But politics alone doesn't explain the paralysis. To understand why change feels so impossible, we have to look beyond policy — and confront the beliefs that keep the system untouchable.

Ideological Barriers: Beliefs That Block Reform

Beneath the politics lies an even deeper barrier: cultural ideology. Public healthcare has become more than a system

— it's a symbol. A symbol of fairness, of shared values, of what it means to be Canadian. But when a system becomes a symbol, questioning it feels like betrayal — and reform becomes nearly impossible.

At the heart of public resistance is a deeply rooted fear: that once profit enters the equation, patient care will suffer. The narrative is familiar — and powerful. If private companies deliver core medical services, they'll prioritize revenue over results. Medicine becomes a marketplace, and patients pay the price.

And while this isn't always the reality — many countries with universal systems successfully balance public and private delivery — the perception persists. Canadians worry that corporate involvement will erode trust, reduce accountability, and deepen inequality. In a country where care is meant to be based on need, not wealth, the two-tier label feels like a betrayal of national values.

The irony? Parts of our current system are already profit driven — just quietly. Diagnostics, labs, surgical contracts, long-term care, and even hospital services are routinely outsourced to private vendors. But these arrangements happen behind the scenes, out of the public eye — and this allows the illusion of a one-tier public system to persist.

As a result, even well intentioned proposals are dismissed before they're understood — because no one is willing to speak openly about what's broken, even when the consequences are undeniable.

Conclusion – Seeing the Barriers Clearly

This chapter isn't about disparaging the system. It's about understanding what lies beneath it — and what's preventing it from evolving. That understanding matters, because most people don't look closely at what's really happening behind the scenes. Instead, they make assumptions, believe the politicians, or cross their fingers and fall back on hope and waiting.

It's a very polite — and very Canadian — response. But once you grasp the depth of the issue, you can decide for yourself whether meaningful reform is truly around the corner, or just another political talking point designed to preserve appearances.

Either way, no matter your stance, you now have a clearer picture of the barriers: the structural limits, legal bottlenecks, quiet workarounds, and deep-rooted cultural resistance. And perhaps most importantly — you now understand the silence that holds it all in place.

This insight isn't theoretical. It's strategic. Because you can't build a modern healthcare access plan — one that actually protects you — without first understanding the forces that work against timely care. No matter how motivated or proactive you are, the system has constraints. Once you know the truth — the contradictions, the limitations, the myths — you can stop waiting for change and start designing around it.

That's not abandoning public healthcare. It's reclaiming agency within it.

Because while delay may be the greatest risk, the deeper injustice is not understanding what's causing it — and not realizing you have the power to choose a different response.

Now, it's time to take the next step — and examine the foundation you're standing on.

Chapter 4

The Limits of Universal Care

We've examined the products. We've examined the structure. Now it's time to confront the gap between them — the space most Canadians rely on for protection.

This chapter is about clarifying what the public system actually delivers — and what it doesn't. Because if you're going to build a modern healthcare strategy, you need to understand the infrastructure you're building around.

Most people assume that Canada's universal healthcare system covers everything they need, when they need it. But that belief is based more on national identity than practical reality. In truth, the system was never designed to deliver fast, flexible, or personalized care. It was built to provide basic, medically necessary services within a budget controlled model.

That distinction matters. Because when you don't know where public coverage ends, you can't see where your risk begins.

In the pages ahead, we'll break down what universal care really delivers — not in theory, but in everyday services. You'll learn what's included, what's missing, and how those gaps quietly shape your options, timeline, and outcomes.

This isn't about criticizing the system. It's about understanding the rules — so you can stop relying on assumptions and start building a plan that actually works in the real world.

Let's take a closer look.

When You Need Answers

Primary care is meant to be the front door of Canada's public healthcare system — the place where most journeys begin. And at first glance, that system appears responsive. You can book an appointment with your family doctor at no cost. Walk into a clinic. Be referred for additional testing or to a specialist. There are no upfront bills, no invoices to process, no credit cards required. On the surface, it feels like things are moving as they should. The structure is in place, and it appears to be working — accessible, familiar, and free.

Until you need the appointment tomorrow. Until fifteen minutes isn't enough. Until the referral takes three to six months to come through. Until your symptoms worsen long before anyone has even looked at your file.

Where the Wait Really Begins

It may be the entry point, but this is also where the system begins to break down. Yes, the visit itself is covered. But what you actually receive is often a rushed appointment, squeezed into a tight schedule sometime within the next 10 business days, delivered with limited continuity and minimal follow-up.

More often than not, you'll spend four times longer in the waiting room than you'll spend in the exam room. The referral process introduces another bottleneck. Even basic diagnostic tests — like X-rays, ultrasounds, bloodwork — can take several weeks to schedule, and the results require another delay, follow-up appointment, another block of time carved out of your already full calendar.

As for advanced imaging — MRIs, CT scans, or anything requiring specialized interpretation — yes, these are technically included in the system. But access depends entirely on urgency. If your case isn't flagged as critical, you'll likely wait months. And before those options are even considered, many physicians are required — or conditioned —

to first rule out less expensive alternatives. That means multiple appointments, repeated testing, and an extended diagnostic timeline that often leaves you in limbo.

For anyone who expects more, these delays are more than frustrating — because without results, nothing else in your life can move forward. So, you're left waiting — not because care doesn't exist, but because access to it is slow, restricted, and largely out of your hands.

That said, for non-urgent concerns — a routine checkup, a mild issue that doesn't impact daily functioning, or a test with no time sensitivity — the wait may feel manageable. If your expectations are low and your timeline is flexible, the system does eventually deliver. But when your life, work, or decisions can't afford to wait, eventually isn't good enough.

When You Need Action

Specialist consults, treatment, and surgery represent the next critical phase in the healthcare journey — the point where diagnosis transitions into intervention, and timely action can directly influence outcomes. This is where speed, coordination, and control matter most.

The Long Wait for Treatment

Moving onward from primary care, eventually — if the process keeps moving forward — you'll get an appointment with a specialist. Once you see that specialist, you'll be added to the surgical schedule. But statistically, it won't happen quickly — and it definitely won't happen on your terms.

According to the Fraser Institute's 2024 report, the median wait time from referral by a general practitioner to the actual delivery of treatment is 30.4 weeks. That's more than half a year between knowing you need help and actually receiving it. And that figure is just the median — many Canadians wait far longer depending on their condition, location, and how the system categorizes their case.

Access to specialists varies dramatically across the country. Geography plays a major role. So does the type of specialty, regional demand, and whether your situation is considered urgent. If your case isn't flagged as critical, you're placed in a queue — and that wait list is rarely short. By design, the system reserves its full attention for emergencies. Preventive, proactive, or performance-sensitive care rarely triggers timely movement.

Surgical procedures are also publicly covered — but the path to the operating room is filled with uncertainty. Unless your situation is classified as urgent, your case can be postponed repeatedly. Operating room capacity is limited.

Cases get re-prioritized. A small influx of emergencies can push your date back by weeks, even months. You may be told your condition isn't serious enough yet — even if it's already disrupting your ability to function.

Waiting for Worsening

This lack of responsiveness doesn't just apply to elective procedures. In many clinical pathways, the system is forced to wait for things to deteriorate before it can act.

Take cancer, for example. In many provinces, pre-cancerous conditions do not qualify for escalated attention. You must wait until the disease officially crosses a diagnostic threshold before intervention is triggered. In other words, the system often needs to see decline before it can respond — even when that decline could have been prevented.

Case Study: Lisa's Story

Lisa, a 48-year-old senior consultant, started experiencing persistent acid reflux and unexplained weight loss. Concerned, she visited her family doctor, who ordered a non-urgent endoscopy. The results showed Barrett's esophagus — a pre-cancerous condition that, in some cases, progresses to esophageal cancer.

Her doctor recommended a referral to a gastroenterologist for surveillance and potentially preventive treatment.

But because Barrett's is considered "watch-and-wait" by provincial standards — not cancer, not urgent — Lisa was placed on a routine referral list.

The wait time? Seven months.

By the time she finally received her next scope, the condition had progressed. A follow-up biopsy confirmed high-grade dysplasia, and shortly after, early-stage adenocarcinoma. She was immediately fast-tracked into cancer care — a path that could have been avoided had action been taken months earlier.

Lisa survived, but her experience left her shaken. The healthcare system didn't lack the ability to treat her — it simply wasn't permitted to act until her condition got worse. Decline was required before intervention.

None of this reflects physician quality. Canadian doctors are among the most skilled, dedicated, and well-trained in the world. They work under immense pressure, often going above and beyond to care for their patients with compassion and expertise.

The issue isn't their capability — it's the structure they're operating within. As explored in Chapter 3, the system is designed for cost containment, not rapid responsiveness. It's overburdened, backlogged, and reactive by default — prioritizing control over agility, policy over patient flow.

Even the most competent physician cannot override systemic constraints: capped billing hours, restricted operating room access, diagnostic bottlenecks, and multi-step referral processes that slow care to a crawl. What you're experiencing as delay is often your doctor encountering a closed door — one they don't have the key to open.

So, while the talent exists and the science has evolved, the delivery remains stalled — leaving both patients and providers stuck in a cycle of deferred action.

For those seeking a higher level of service — faster timelines, greater consistency, and coordinated care — this reactive model simply can't deliver. It's not built to meet those expectations. And the moment your needs extend beyond a basic appointment or standard test, that gap becomes glaringly obvious.

When You Need Broader Support

Mental health, maternal care, medications, and rural access are essential areas of support that extend beyond acute treatment — and yet, in Canada's public system, these services are often fragmented, inconsistently covered, or difficult to access when and where they're needed most. The further your needs stray from hospital based intervention, the more fragile the system becomes.

Take mental health. While public programs exist, they're notoriously patchy. Waitlists are long, and most care happens at the primary level — not with psychologists or licensed therapists, but with overburdened GPs. If you want speed, continuity, or meaningful choice, you'll likely be paying out of pocket.

Maternal care offers another example. Support is strong during delivery, but access to prenatal care, postpartum monitoring, and lactation resources can vary widely — especially outside of urban centers.

Case Study: Distance as a Barrier — Rural Realities

When Caleb, a 52-year-old construction manager in northern Ontario, began experiencing cardiac symptoms, his local clinic referred him for testing — three hours away. The earliest available appointment was eight weeks out, in a city with no direct public transportation. To make it work, he had to miss two full days of work, arrange for a hotel overnight, and coordinate his follow-up care from a distance. The cost wasn't just time — it was disruption.

He's far from alone. According to the Canadian Institute for Health Information, Canadians living in rural or remote areas face wait times two to four times longer than those in urban centers — along with significantly greater travel burdens for specialist consultations, diagnostic imaging, therapy, and surgical procedures.

Even when care is technically covered, geography becomes its own barrier. Access isn't just about cost — it's about proximity, coordination, and the ability to act when time matters.

These types of access challenges — whether geographic, financial, or structural — are frustrating enough when you're trying to stay healthy. But they become even more consequential after illness, injury, or major surgery, when the need for ongoing support remains high but the system you rely on starts to fade away.

And that's where the next breakdown happens — not at diagnosis, but at what comes next.

When You Need Recovery

Post-operative care, rehabilitation, and long-term support make up the critical — and often underestimated — final phase of the healthcare journey. This is where healing either accelerates or stalls, where setbacks can be avoided, and where sustained progress depends not just on clinical expertise, but on continued access, thoughtful coordination, and consistent follow-through.

Yet this is precisely where the public system begins to fade.

Once the acute issue is addressed — the surgery completed, the condition stabilized — the system effectively steps back. In the eyes of the public model, the urgent part is over, and your case is closed. But for you, recovery is just beginning.

Case Study: Recovery Not Included

After a skiing accident left Marc — a 48-year-old architect and avid cyclist — with a torn ACL and months of rehab ahead, he assumed recovery would be straightforward. The surgery was covered. So was the hospital stay. But everything after that? Not so much. His follow-up care was minimal, and the public rehab program offered just four in-person sessions over six weeks. To get the support he actually needed — weekly physio, hydrotherapy, and gait correction — Marc had to go fully private. The price tag: over $7,000.

Rehabilitation services may exist through hospitals or provincial programs, but they're often reserved for only the most severe or complex cases. Even then, the waitlists can stretch for weeks or months. The actual time allotted for publicly funded rehab is brief — a handful of sessions that may barely scratch the surface of what's required to restore full function. It's a start, not a solution.

Outpatient rehab, in-home physiotherapy, occupation-al therapy, assistive devices — the kinds of support that bridge the gap between medical discharge and real-world recovery — are typically only partially covered, if at all. In most cases, the onus falls squarely on the patient to arrange follow-up care, coordinate logistics, fund the necessary support, or go without altogether.

This is the point where many people expect the system to keep showing up for them — and discover that it won't. The moment you're discharged, the safety net begins to disappear. In the system's eyes, you've been treated. But in reality, you may still be far from functional — physically, mentally, or emotionally. You may be cleared, but you're not yet capable.

And what happens next is largely up to you.

When You Need Medication

Recovery isn't the only stage where public support thins out. Even the most essential, ongoing needs — like access to prescription medications — can expose just how limited that support really is.

Most Canadians assume that serious medical conditions automatically come with comprehensive drug coverage. But just like rehab, income protection, and home-based care, prescription medication in Canada is governed by a complex maze of limitations, exclusions, and delays. And when those gaps appear, the consequences are anything but theoretical.

The Truth About Public Drug Coverage

Drug coverage is one of the most misunderstood elements of our healthcare system. While medications are subsidized in Canada, eligibility and scope vary dramatically by province — and the fine print matters.

In Ontario, for example, public drug benefits are largely reserved for those under 24, over 65, or receiving social assistance. That leaves the majority of working age adults without public coverage.

And even when you qualify, the list of covered medications isn't exhaustive. Ontario's formulary includes thousands of drugs, but many newer, more advanced, or higher cost options are excluded. That includes biologics, off-label uses, brand-name alternatives, and medications sourced internationally. If your treatment doesn't align with the system's criteria, you may be forced to pay out-of-pocket — or endure a drawn-out trial of less effective drugs first.

The In-Patient Loophole

One of the most significant, yet least understood, drug coverage gaps is what's known as the in-patient loophole.

Some of the most expensive and cutting-edge treatments — particularly cancer therapies — are only fully covered if administered in a hospital.

For example, if a cancer drug is delivered intravenously during an inpatient stay, it's typically funded. But if the same drug is prescribed in oral form, coverage often disappears — shifting the entire financial burden to the patient.

Case Study: The Coverage Cutoff

When Raj, a 61-year-old small business owner, was diagnosed with stage II lymphoma, his oncology team recommended a new oral chemotherapy drug — one that had shown excellent results with fewer side effects than traditional IV treatments.

The problem? Because the medication was designed for at-home use, it wasn't covered by Ontario's public plan. Had Raj received a comparable drug via IV during a hospital stay, the entire treatment would have been fully funded. But because he was stable enough to remain outpatient, the $6,000-per-month cost became his responsibility.

This wasn't an experimental therapy. It was approved by Health Canada and part of standard oncology care — just not administered inside a hospital. Raj's options? Drain his retirement savings to access the best treatment, or settle for an older, less effective alternative that was covered, but came with harsher side effects and a longer recovery time.

This isn't a rare exception. With more modern treatments designed for outpatient or oral delivery, it's becoming increasingly common. And for patients like Raj, it means making impossible choices between financial stability and optimal care.

This story isn't an exception — it's a warning. A reminder that even essential care like medication can fall through the cracks.

From Public Limitations to Private Possibilities

This chapter wasn't about finding fault. It was about revealing the truth — getting clear on what the public system actually delivers, and what it doesn't. Even when access is delayed, restricted, or out of reach, this is still the system you're expected to rely on. But if you don't understand its true limits — or recognize where it no longer meets your needs — you can't plan with any real precision.

Yes, the public model offers critical, high quality care. But it was designed to serve the population as a whole, not to offer individual control or customization. The delays, the exclusions, the reactive structure — these aren't failures in execution. They are features of design.

If you're looking for anything more than the basic, then relying solely on this system comes with access risk. Whether it can't deliver what you need, or you just can't afford to wait, the consequences are significant. You don't just need care eventually. You need it predictably, efficiently, and with enough control to protect your time, choices, and outcomes. And as it stands, the public model can't deliver that.

From a planning perspective, public care should be seen as Plan A — the starting point, not the full solution. Now that you understand where that foundation ends, you're ready to build beyond it. Because if you want care that meets modern expectations — faster timelines, consistent follow through, and access on your terms — that next layer doesn't exist in the public model.

It exists in the private one.

In Chapter 5, we map out what that landscape actually looks like — the reality, the legality, and the strategic value of building private healthcare into your plan. Not as a replacement, but as a powerful, protective extension of it.

Chapter 5

Understanding Canada's Private Healthcare Landscape

If the public system can't deliver when it counts — what's your next move?

By now, you've seen the reality most Canadians never fully grasp, universal healthcare, while high quality when accessible, isn't designed to meet modern expectations. It's reactive, slow, and limited — not because the doctors aren't skilled, but because the structure can't keep up.

In Chapter 3, we explored the legislative barriers — the ideological resistance and the legal limits that restrict private payment for publicly insured services. That left many readers wondering: If the law prohibits private care, how does private care exist at all?

That's exactly what this chapter will answer.

Despite what many believe — and what we explored earlier
— a parallel system has not only persisted, it has steadily
expanded. Not through loopholes, but through lawful-
ly designed workarounds that quietly operate within the
framework of the Canada Health Act. These aren't viola-
tions of the law. They are strategic responses to its limitations — shaped by provincial discretion, evolving demand,
and a growing list of services no longer fully covered by the
public system.

This chapter will walk you through that reality — what's
legal, what's available, and what's already working for
thousands of Canadians who can't afford to wait. Because
if you want timely, customized care, it doesn't start with
hope. It starts with strategy.

To understand how that strategy is possible — and why
private options exist despite legislative restrictions — it
helps to step back. The roots of private care in Canada run
deeper than most people realize, and the system we have
today is shaped as much by what was grandfathered in as
by what was later legislated.

A Quick Look Back: How Private Insurance Took Root in Canada

Private healthcare in Canada isn't new — it actually predates the public system. Before the Canada Health Act

was introduced in the 1980s, healthcare coverage varied widely by province, and many Canadians relied on private insurance to cover services that weren't locally available or publicly funded.

When the Act came into effect, it standardized public funding for what was deemed medically necessary. But it didn't eliminate private care — it simply redefined its role. Private services weren't banned; they were pushed to the sidelines, permitted only when they didn't directly compete with insured public offerings.

The result? A quiet two-tier system. One tier is highly visible: the public infrastructure most Canadians know. The other is more discreet — a layer of private care that's quietly coexisted alongside the public model for decades.

Yet despite its long-standing presence, many Canadians are still unaware of this parallel system. That lack of awareness has allowed misconceptions to persist — including the false belief that private care is new, foreign, or incompatible with Canadian values. In reality, private healthcare has always played a role in our system, quietly filling gaps the public sector chose not to cover.

The next section unpacks how that role has been shaped over time — not by accident, but by design — through

policies that have defined, limited, and ultimately legit-
imized the private layer we see today.

Who Decides What's Covered?

At the core of Canada's healthcare structure is a division
of authority. The federal government sets the funding expectations through the Canada Health Act, but it's the
provinces that determine how those expectations are met.
That means the definition of medically necessary varies
across jurisdictions. What qualifies in one province may
not in another.

This provincial discretion is what creates the space — and
ambiguity — for private care to flourish. If a service isn't
insured, it can be offered and billed privately, without vio-
lating federal law. This is how private providers have continued to expand: not by breaking rules, but by working
within them and simply meeting growing demand.

But to really understand how that space exists — and why
it continues to widen — we need to look more closely at
the phrase that underpins it all: medically necessary.

What Does Medically Necessary Actually Mean?

These two words determine what's covered by the public
system — and by extension, what can't legally be offered
or billed privately. But here's the issue: the term has never

been clearly or consistently defined. Its interpretation is left to each province — and often shaped by the political climate of the day.

Decades ago, that ambiguity gave rise to private offerings like health and dental plans — services that fell outside the scope of insured care. But in more recent years, as public systems have struggled to keep pace with demand, and governments have quietly reduced or rationed services, the definition has been stretched further. The result? A growing ecosystem of care that operates legally — yet often tests the outer limits of what's considered publicly insurable.

The Canada Health Act hasn't changed. But the ground level reality has, with fewer services, longer waits, more gaps. And it's in those gaps that private care has expanded — not as a replacement for public care, but as a response to its limitations. Faster, more flexible, and increasingly essential.

How Private Clinics Operate Within the Law

So, the growing network of private clinics in Canada doesn't exist because of loopholes — they exist because of limits. Limits on what the public system covers. Limits on how quickly care is delivered. And limits on what physicians can offer within the insured framework.

The legal foundation for private care is simple: the Canada Health Act governs what provinces must insure — not what healthcare providers can offer. If a service isn't covered under a provincial plan, there's no law preventing a private clinic from offering it — or charging for it. And the more the public system decreases what's covered, the more the opportunities become available.

That's why we now see a growing, legally sanctioned ecosystem of private clinics operating across the country. Some work entirely outside the public system. Others use hybrid models, referring patients back into the insured stream where appropriate. Some cater to individuals; others are built for employers. But they're all responding to the same thing: unmet demand.

These clinics aren't duplicating core hospital or physician services. Like any other private offering, they're simply delivering what the public model doesn't: longer appointments, faster diagnostics, flexible scheduling, and advanced or specialized care.

This isn't a workaround. It's a lawful, strategic response to a public system under pressure — and it's becoming an essential part of care for those who can't afford to wait.

Legal Challenges and Misconceptions

Have these clinics been challenged legally? Yes — but not successfully shut down. The most well-known case, Cambie Surgeries Corporation v. British Columbia (2020), centered on whether patients have a constitutional right to pay for faster access to care. The court upheld restrictions on dual billing, but it didn't outlaw private care, reinforcing the fact that provincial governments retain the right to regulate how and when private services can be delivered.

Translation? Private healthcare is still very much legal and increasingly important. But it's not consistently available — and where you live matters more than ever.

Not All Provinces Play by the Same Rules

Because healthcare is administered by provinces, your access to private services depends heavily on where you live.

In provinces like Quebec, Ontario, Alberta, and Saskatchewan, private clinics offering diagnostics, consults, and surgeries are more visible and accessible. In others, like BC or Manitoba, tighter regulations make access more limited. Even within provinces, there's variation in how services are offered and what's allowed.

This is why location-aware healthcare planning is essential. Knowing what's legal — and where — is one of the biggest advantages in building a personalized strategy.

The Shift Was Driven by Demand and Quietly Endorsed by Policy

Private clinics didn't appear overnight. Their growth was gradual — and driven by unmet needs. Ontario led the shift, not through political declarations, but through practical realities. Professionals with the means to pay for faster care began seeking alternatives: shorter waits, greater control, and more responsive service than the public system could offer.

As that model proved viable, other provinces quietly followed. And while no government stood up to actively champion private expansion, none stood in the way either. Because legally, they didn't have to. As long as these clinics operated outside the public billing system and avoided core insured services, they remained within legal bounds — and government remained neutral.

In fact, some might argue the shift hasn't just been tolerated — it's been strategically convenient. Provincial leaders understand that the public system can no longer meet full demand. Services are quietly trimmed or reclassified. In Ontario, for example, an ambulance ride now comes with a bill, and routine Vitamin D testing is no longer covered. As the list of exclusions grows, private options move in to fill the gaps — solving access issues without requiring the government to take an overt political stance. It's a kind of passive endorsement: allow private care to expand, let the public benefit, and avoid publicly acknowledging the shift.

Ontario made this tacit relationship more explicit in 2023. With waitlists surging and system strain deepening, the government passed Bill 60 (Your Health Act), allowing private clinics to legally perform publicly funded procedures. It marked a turning point: not just in private sector expansion, but in the province's willingness to formalize the role of private providers in public care delivery.

What began as a quiet, cautious workaround has since evolved into a high level alternative to public care. This isn't a loophole. It's a response — one shaped not by ideology, but by demand, practicality, and systemic necessity. And that demand is only accelerating.

The Rise of Private Surgical Clinics

One of the clearest — and most visible — examples of how private care operates legally in Canada is the steady growth of independent surgical clinics. These facilities offer procedures like cataract surgeries, orthopedic interventions, colonoscopies, biopsies, and more. They're typically designed to manage lower-risk cases and relieve pressure on overburdened hospitals — often delivering care faster, more efficiently, and with fewer delays than the public stream.

What makes these clinics especially noteworthy isn't just what they offer, but how clearly they embody the legal principles we've already explored. They matter because their existence is a clear signal to anyone who questions the legality of private care in Canada. Not only is private delivery of healthcare permitted but it is being increasingly relied upon as a practical solution to public system strain. These clinics don't operate in a legal grey zone. Their existence is rooted in the same structure that underpins other forms of private care: staying outside the boundaries of insured services or operating under provincial discretion. And in doing so, they offer a blueprint for how healthcare delivery is quietly — but significantly — shifting in Canada towards private solutions.

Depending on the province, surgical clinics tend to follow one of three models, but regardless of the model, the common denominator is speed, flexibility, and control. For anyone managing a full plate, these clinics aren't about luxury — they're about logistics. They offer timely care that meets real-world needs and helps avoid unnecessary downtime.

At first glance, surgical clinics may seem like just another example of private care. And in many ways, they are. But they also reveal something more: how provinces are strategically leaning into these models — not by accident, but by design. As demand continues to outpace what the public system can deliver, these clinics are expanding quietly, legally, and with increasing impact.

Legal Avenues for Timely Surgical Care

What's changing in Canadian healthcare isn't the law itself — it's how provinces are applying their discretion to meet rising surgical demand without expanding public infrastructure.

As pressure builds, provincial governments are increasingly turning to private surgical delivery — not as a political statement, but as a practical necessity. The legal framework permits it. The demand compels it. And the result is a growing, legitimate layer of private care operating quietly across the country.

Provinces are using a few key mechanisms to enable this shift.

In Alberta, Saskatchewan, Manitoba, Ontario and Quebec, governments are contracting private surgical clinics to perform publicly funded procedures. In these cases, the government pays — not the patient — and while the care is delivered in private facilities, it follows public rules. The goal is to reduce wait times without the need for costly new hospital infrastructure. This model is legal, expanding, and one of the quietest ways private care is becoming mainstream.

In some provinces — particularly Quebec, and to a lesser extent Alberta and Ontario — patients can legally pay out of pocket for surgeries, but only under specific conditions. The procedure must be uninsured by the public plan, the physician and clinic must have opted out of the public billing system, and the province must permit private billing in those cases. While B.C. and Ontario maintain tighter restrictions, workarounds still exist — especially for procedures that are medically necessary but not considered urgent by public standards.

Other clinics operate entirely outside the insured system. They offer services like cosmetic or elective orthopedic surgeries, vision correction, or diagnostics that aren't covered by provincial plans. Some also provide premium add-ons like private recovery suites, advanced imaging, or faster turnaround times. Because these services were never included in public coverage, delivering them privately doesn't violate any law.

Though these delivery models differ, they share one critical commonality: they are all legal, and they're all part of how healthcare access is evolving in Canada.

Yet despite how deeply rooted these clinics are in provincial policy, most Canadians have no idea they exist. Even as governments rely on private partners to help clear surgical backlogs, the public narrative rarely acknowledges their role.

Understanding this isn't just useful — it's strategic. These clinics aren't fringe workarounds. For professionals, decision-makers, and anyone who can't afford to wait, they represent not just an option, but a viable and increasingly necessary part of healthcare planning.

Why Most People Still Don't Know What's Available

Despite their legality and growing role, most private services remain virtually invisible — not because they're inaccessible, but because they're under-promoted, under-navigated, and rarely acknowledged. The system doesn't endorse what it doesn't fund, and that silence keeps most Canadians in the dark.

But beyond politics, there's a deeper reason these services stay off the radar: many Canadians are still anchored to an outdated belief — that the public system will support them when it matters most.

That belief, while once justified, no longer reflects today's reality. And as long as people assume the public model will meet their needs, they won't question delays, denials, or dead ends. They'll wait. They'll adapt. They'll settle.

But thousands of Canadians have already stepped outside that narrative — using private services legally and proactively to reduce downtime, regain control, and stay ahead of disruption.

To do the same, the first shift isn't tactical. It's mental. It starts with acknowledging that the system isn't failing because people are doing something wrong — it's failing because it was never built to handle this level of demand. And whether or not governments say it aloud, they're increasingly leaning on the private sector to close the gaps — by quietly limiting coverage and trimming services without formally declaring it as policy.

Even so, private care in Canada remains poorly understood — especially among those who would benefit most. Most public physicians aren't permitted to refer patients to private clinics. Most private providers operate with minimal marketing or visibility. And there's no central database or directory to show what's legally available — and where.

The result? Services that are lawful, expanding, and effective — but invisible to the average Canadian.

When most people hear private healthcare, they think of group benefits — drug plans, dental cleanings, vision coverage, maybe a massage. And yes, those are technically private. But they only scratch the surface.

The kind of private care that actually moves the needle includes services operating entirely outside the insured boundaries of the public system. And for people who value their time, performance, and peace of mind, this is where the real leverage lives.

Understanding this landscape isn't just about awareness — it's about strategy.

From Legal Landscape to Personal Strategy

This chapter wasn't just about proving that private care is legal — it was about showing you what's possible. What's available. And why that matters more than ever.

For years, private healthcare in Canada has been misunderstood — seen as inaccessible, unethical, or irrelevant. But those perceptions no longer reflect reality. The real issue hasn't been legality. It's been visibility. Most people don't use private options not because they can't — but because they don't know they exist.

Now you do.

Private care in Canada isn't an exception or indulgence. It's a lawful, expanding, and increasingly essential layer of support — not in opposition to public care, but in response to its limitations. For professionals, business owners, caregivers, and anyone managing multiple responsibilities, this second layer isn't optional. It's strategic. Because when your timeline matters, when downtime has consequences, and when being stuck in the queue isn't a viable option — the plan can't be wait and see.

But awareness alone isn't enough. Knowing what's legal is only the first step. What matters now is how you use that knowledge — how you build a plan that doesn't just react to the system, but works around it.

That's where we go next.

In Chapter 6, we move from concept to construction. You'll learn how to build the first layer of your healthcare access strategy — using tools that are legal, available, and already in use by thousands of Canadians who can't afford to wait. From health benefits to private clinics, diagnostics, telehealth, and more, we'll explore what works, where it fits, and how it all connects.

Because real protection doesn't begin in a crisis. It begins with structure.

Let's build it.

Chapter 6

The First Floor: Building on Your Foundation

You've seen the blueprint. Now it's time to start building.

In the last chapter, we exposed the truth: private care in Canada isn't illegal, unethical, or inaccessible — it's just underused. And for those who can't afford to wait, it's becoming not just an option, but a necessity.

What comes next is the shift from awareness to action — from understanding what exists to knowing how to use it.

This chapter introduces the first layer of your Plan B: the foundational services that offer speed, control, and clarity when the public system stalls. We'll start with the most familiar and accessible — health and dental plans, primary care clinics, diagnostics, telehealth, at-home testing, and specialized providers. Some of these may already be part of your life. Others may have been hidden from view until now.

These services don't replace public care — they reinforce it. Think of them as your first floor: a functional, flexible base that supports real-time access, better outcomes, and fewer setbacks. They're not perfect. They won't solve every problem. But they represent your first real leverage point — the difference between reacting late and acting early.

Like any structure, real protection is built layer by layer. Let's put the first brick in place.

What Benefits Plans Can Do — and What They Can't

For most Canadians, the first introduction to private healthcare support doesn't come through a clinic — it comes through a benefits plan. Whether employer-provided or individually purchased, these plans cover a familiar list of services: dental, vision, physiotherapy, chiropractic care, massage, mental health, prescription drugs, and sometimes disability and critical illness. They're often referred to as extended health benefits or supplemental plans — not because they replace the public system, but because they expand on what it offers.

We reviewed these plans in more depth back in Chapter 2, so we won't spend too much time on them here, but it's worth reinforcing their role in the overall strategy. They're popular and they're helpful, but here's the problem: most people assume these benefits are comprehensive protection. They're not.

All plans include maximums and exclusions. You may get $500 a year for physiotherapy, or $1500 for prescriptions — but those caps often aren't enough to fund real recovery or consistent support. Coverage for drugs also exclude newer, brand or specialty medications without prior authorization. Dental plans may not include major restorative work. Vision, disability and critical illness are basic, and there is no assistance beyond reimbursement for the expenses or visit.

That's why benefits, while helpful, can't be mistaken for a strategy. They won't get you a faster MRI. They won't move your surgical timeline forward. They won't provide access to a specialist when your referral is stuck in a three-month queue. And they certainly won't help you coordinate care across multiple providers, locations, or systems. They're partial, misunderstood, and overestimated.

That said, they're still valuable — especially when used strategically. Knowing what's available, how to access it, and how to supplement public care can help reduce costs, prevent setbacks, and support continuity. But they're not the entire floor. They're a layer that sits on top of the public foundation, one that can stretch only so far without the rest of your plan to support it.

So, when nominal expense reimbursement isn't the only concern — when you're looking for real-time answers — that's where primary care comes in.

Primary Care: Access That Moves When You Do

If benefits plans represent the most common access point to private care, primary care clinics represent the most foundational upgrade. These clinics exist across Canada — some are branded as executive health, others as family medicine, wellness, or integrative practices. But what they share is a reorientation around time, access, and relationship.

In the public system, most family doctors carry rosters of 1,500 to 2,000 patients. Appointments are often limited to 10–15 minutes. Continuity can be inconsistent, especially in large practices. And when issues require more time, investigation, or context, the default response is often: let's wait and see.

Private clinics shift that model. Appointments are longer. Same-day and next-day bookings are common. Physicians have more time to investigate, listen, and connect dots that might otherwise be missed. Many include annual exams, health assessments, lifestyle tracking, and direct follow-up.

Some offer coordination of care — helping you move faster through preventative care or diagnostics.

For people with complex lives, high demand on their time, or layered health needs, this kind of relationship is invaluable. It's not just about speed — it's about clarity, context, and forward motion. When something feels off, you're seen. When something changes, you're not waiting three weeks to talk about it. And when next steps are needed, you have someone to provide referrals or requisitions immediately.

Still, private primary care is not emergency medicine. It doesn't replace hospitals, specialists, or surgical teams. It won't guarantee you a private room or a shorter hospital stay, nor can it get you in to see a specialist faster. But it does give you a base layer of control — the ability to act sooner, track progress, and maintain momentum in a system that otherwise stalls.

Case Study: When Private Care Meets a Public Roadblock

Mario and his wife have relied on a private primary care clinic for years. They appreciate the consistency of seeing the same doctor, the ease of booking same- or next-day appointments, and the thoroughness of their annual assessments. Their physician has become a trusted partner in managing everything from cholesterol to mental health and they like the extras the clinic offers.

But when Mario's wife went in for a routine screening and her doctor flagged a suspicious mass, they hit a wall. The clinic quickly ordered a scan, but when it confirmed that a biopsy was needed, they were told it had to be done in the public system — because it was now classified as medically necessary. That meant re-entering the queue with everyone else, waiting weeks for the procedure.

It was a stark reminder: even the best private care doesn't create shortcuts for certain services. It improves access, speed, and relationship — but some doors still only open through the public system.

Diagnostics: The Waiting Game, Rewritten

If primary care is the engine of access, diagnostics are the fuel. Without clear, timely testing, even the best clinical teams can't move forward. And in Canada, diagnostics are one of the most common — and consequential — bottlenecks.

X-rays, ultrasounds, MRIs, CT scans, ECGs, stress tests, bloodwork — these are the tools that reveal what's happening beneath the surface. And in the public system, they're technically covered. But as you've seen, access depends on urgency. If your condition isn't flagged as critical, you may be waiting weeks or months. Even routine blood-work can take time to schedule. Results often require follow-up. And each layer — booking, testing, analysis, consultation — adds more delay.

Private diagnostics compress that timeline. In most major cities, and increasingly in suburban and rural areas, private imaging clinics and labs offer access to testing on your schedule — not the system's. You can book an MRI this week, not next season. You can get bloodwork done tomorrow, with results in hand before your next appointment. And you can do it without bouncing between providers or departments.

For performance focused individuals, this kind of speed doesn't just relieve anxiety — it preserves momentum. It means you're not sidelined for months waiting to know what's next. It allows you to act, adjust, and recover faster. And in many cases, it allows your team — public or private — to work with clearer data, sooner.

Case Study: The Speed of Answers vs. the Pace of Action

Lena, an avid runner in Calgary, had been experiencing a recurring hip pain for months. Her public referral for imaging kept getting delayed, pushing her recovery further into the future. Tired of waiting, she booked a private MRI and had results within 10 days. The imaging confirmed a tendon issue — not serious, but enough to explain the pain and require rehab.

For Lena the speed meant avoiding unnecessary time off work. But while private diagnostics got her the answer, she still had to coordinate her treatment through the public system. This introduced new wait times and hurdles and illustrates the limitations. Private imaging got her moving — but it didn't remove every barrier.

That's the central tension with this primary level of care: it's excellent for getting answers quicker — but answers aren't action. If the results lead to surgery, complex treatment, or medically necessary intervention, the next step often returns you to the public system. In that way, diagnostics are a powerful accelerant — but not always a fast track to resolution.

At-Home Testing: Access Without Appointments

Not all diagnostics require a lab coat or a clinic. In recent years, a wave of at-home testing services has expanded what Canadians can access from the privacy of their own homes — often without needing a doctor's referral or a single step into the public system.

These include everything from colon cancer screening kits and STI tests to genetic health panels, microbiome analysis, pap alternatives, and food sensitivity testing. Some offer simple results with consumer-friendly language; others provide physician reviewed reports, digital consultations, or referrals if needed.

What makes these tools powerful isn't just convenience — it's autonomy. They allow people to act on curiosity, concern, or family history without delay. They support early insight, especially when public waitlists for non-urgent testing can stretch for months. And they help monitor health trends, identify risks, and seek care earlier — sometimes before symptoms appear.

But like all tools on the first floor, they have limits.

These tests don't replace clinical care. They're not diagnostic proof — they're information. Positive results often require follow-up through formal providers, and negative results don't always tell the full story. Accuracy can vary depending on the type of test and the provider.

Still, for those looking to gain more insight between checkups or fill in gaps left by the system, at-home testing can be a powerful layer of intelligence. Not as a replacement for face-to-face care — but as a bridge to it.

The Role of Specialized Clinics

Beyond diagnostics and primary care, there's a tier of private services designed not just to treat illness, but to optimize health or focus on specific wellness issues. Executive clinics, longevity practices, performance and hormone centers, fertility clinics, gender based testing, holistic, functional and integrative medical centres all offer expanded access — but in different ways.

These aren't emergency services. They don't replace hospitals or specialists. What they do offer is depth: specialized assessments, broader testing, proactive strategies, and highly personalized care plans. Many include physical exams, genetic testing, nutrition support, mental health services, and access to allied health professionals — all under one roof.

For anyone balancing leadership, family, and personal demands — these clinics can function as both quarterback and checkpoint. They help monitor risk, identify changes early, and track progress over time. They're not about treating what's broken — they're about preventing breakdown in the first place.

That said, they don't cover everything. If you need surgery, hospitalization, or complex intervention, they'll refer you — just like any other provider. But they do give you something rare in Canadian healthcare: a proactive, data-informed approach to staying well.

Telehealth: Convenience, Not Comprehensiveness

If there's one private service that exploded in visibility over the past few years, it's telehealth. Once a niche offering, it's now a mainstay in both public and private care. And while it offers incredible convenience, it also comes with limits.

Virtual platforms allow you to consult with physicians, renew prescriptions, get advice, and in some cases, receive referrals and requisitions — all without leaving your home or office. For anyone with a busy schedule, this is a game-changer. It reduces friction. It keeps care accessible. And it solves for many of the day-to-day questions that otherwise get pushed to the back burner.

Case Study: When Virtual Care Reaches Its Limit

Kevin, a consultant who travels across Canada for work, relies on a virtual care app for managing routine issues — prescription renewals, skin rashes, and even flu symptoms. While on a trip to Winnipeg, he developed a dry cough that worsened over the week. Through the app, he spoke with a physician and got a prescription, but when the symptoms escalated, he was told to visit a walk-in clinic or emergency room for further testing.

The convenience was invaluable — but when the issue became more complex, Kevin hit the edge of what telehealth could offer. It got him started — but couldn't carry him through to the finish line.

Telehealth is best understood as a front door — not a full house. It can initiate care but rarely completes it. Complex cases, diagnostic testing, physical exams, procedures, and hands-on follow-up all require in-person support. And when escalation is needed, telehealth providers will always direct you back to the public system.

That's not a flaw — it's just a reminder. Like the other products and services that form the first layer of your plan, telehealth is a tool, not a complete solution. Used well, it saves time, reduces stress, and helps maintain continuity. Used in isolation, it can create blind spots.

Layer One, Not the Whole Plan

Now that we've reviewed the most familiar services — benefits plans, primary care, diagnostics, specialty clinics, at-home testing, and telehealth — you have a clear view of how to build the first layer of your healthcare access strategy. Together, these services restore momentum, reduce wait times, and help you regain control when the public system can't keep up.

But let's be clear: one preventative layer isn't enough.

When your needs shift from routine to urgent, the first level can only carry you so far. No combination of benefits, diagnostics, or virtual visits will help when you need surgery or advanced treatment because you now face structural limitations that block access. Without expanding your strategy to consider this inevitable barrier, you will still hit walls, face queues, and be at the mercy of a system that can't move fast enough.

So, the first floor is your foundation — but protection only becomes complete when you build upwards. That's where we go next.

In Chapter 7, we enter the second floor: the level where concierge medicine becomes the focus, creating real-time clarity, coordination and access in these highly consequential moments. It's where time sensitive care is activated — not passively hoped for. The is the layer most Canadians never plan for until it's too late.

Let's keep building.

Chapter 7

The Second Floor: Precision Access and Urgent Care Strategy

Some health events are urgent — and this is exactly what the second floor of your healthcare strategy is designed to deal with.

When routine care gives way to something more serious, and you don't have the luxury of waiting for answers or treatment, your plan must be ready to respond — matching access to urgency. This next level isn't a luxury; it's a dedicated layer designed for moments when delay simply isn't an option.

The first floor handled the everyday: proactive checkups, diagnostics, virtual care, and basic coordination. But when those services uncover something serious, systemic barriers send you right back into the public system — where the critical wait begins.

That's why the next tier matters so much. Built around the navigation provided by concierge medicine, it's not about perks. It's about speed and clarity — a comprehensive system that activates when your timeline tightens, your condition escalates, or your needs become more complex.

It doesn't replace the foundation beneath it. It builds on top of it — turning readiness into responsiveness, and passive coverage into real control. This is the second floor of your Plan B — the route you take when Plan A slows down, stalls, or disappears entirely.

We're all in agreement that Canada's public system offers excellent care — but this only applies when you can access what you need in time. And for most Canadians, outside of the ER, this is the exception, not the rule.

That's why this upper level has become a vital — and often non-negotiable — component of modern healthcare planning. It's not about rejecting the public system. It's about stepping in when the system can't move fast enough to protect what matters most.

Let's keep building.

The Role of the Concierge

When care can't wait, clarity and coordination matter most. That's where a medical concierge team comes in — not as a premium add-on, but as the architect of timely, effective treatment.

Unlike your family doctor, a concierge isn't just a referral source. They're your personal healthcare strategist. They gather your medical records, assess your situation, identify next steps, and open doors the public system often keeps closed. They're the reason some patients avoid unnecessary surgeries, secure faster second opinions, or access international care when local options fall short.

If the first layer of your healthcare plan is preventative care, then think of the concierge as the elevator — moving you swiftly to the second floor and helping you access advanced care when the stakes are highest. They don't just advise. They act — immediately.

Drawing on trusted national and international networks, deep knowledge of Canada's public and private systems, and years of logistical experience, concierge teams coordinate diagnostics, connect with surgical teams, and manage the moving parts. Many also support hybrid approaches — combining public coverage with private options to accelerate access.

For example, most Canadians don't know that an employer can legally pay for private surgery — but the patient themselves cannot. That kind of nuance is exactly what a skilled concierge navigates with precision. In short, if you want real access to everything the second floor has to offer, a medical concierge isn't optional — they're essential.

Let's take a closer look at what that includes.

Diagnostic Clarity

Across modern healthcare systems — including Canada's — diagnostic errors are more common than most people realize. Well documented medical studies estimate that 5 to 15 percent of diagnoses are either incorrect or delayed. The consequences are serious: missed cancers, misread cardiac conditions, and chronic illnesses dismissed as anxiety or stress.

Why does this happen?

Systemic delays create long waits for imaging and specialist referrals. Short appointments often lead to incomplete evaluations. Fragmented medical records prevent providers from seeing the full picture. And in an overburdened system, even skilled physicians may lack the time or tools to investigate complex symptoms thoroughly. As a result, family doctors are increasingly expected to make specialized diagnoses — not because it's ideal, but because the wait to see a specialist has become unsustainably long. And even when a consult finally happens, the data informing it may already be outdated. Combine that with siloed records and rushed evaluations, and it's easy to see how errors — or missed opportunities — can happen.

Case Study: From Misdiagnosis to Clarity in 10 Days

Andreas, 52, Executive, Windsor - Andreas was told he needed a knee replacement, but the diagnosis didn't sit right. Through a concierge coordinated second opinion, a specialist reviewed his MRI and confirmed the real issue was a complex ligament injury — treatable without surgery. He started a targeted rehab plan within a week.

This is where medical concierge services become indispensable.

With a deep understanding of the public system's limitations, a concierge team can act quickly. They request your full file within days, assess diagnostics already completed, and arrange further testing through private clinics to clarify your results — often within a week. But that's only the first step.

Second Opinion

Once clarity begins to emerge, the next priority is verification. Because when time, certainty, and outcomes are at stake, a second opinion isn't just helpful — it's essential.

A medical concierge can secure access to multiple world class specialists — in Canada or abroad — to ensure diagnostic accuracy. This level of second opinion can uncover alternative treatments, prevent unnecessary procedures, and restore your confidence to move forward — or provide a critical course correction before valuable time is lost.

Case Study: Biopsy in Days, Not Months

Susan, 56, Philanthropist, Caledon - After returning from Florida with concerning imaging results, Susan was told she'd have to wait over a month for a biopsy. Her concierge team had the procedure arranged and completed within ten days at a private clinic — along with a surgical consult to review next steps.

Trying to achieve this through the public system is virtually impossible. Wait times for a single specialist consultation can stretch from three to twelve months. Most primary care providers won't issue a second referral, and a third is unheard of. In this respect, the concierge is not just helpful — they're essential.

They coordinate expert case reviews, fast-track advanced testing like MRIs or genetic screening, and connect you with leading specialists who provide integrated, evidence-based recommendations — quickly. And to be clear, these aren't the generic summaries or algorithm-generated reports offered as add-ons to critical illness policies or virtual care apps. These are real physicians, reviewing your records in detail, answering your questions, and guiding your decisions — face-to-face. Because you're not just a file. You're a participant. And when the stakes are high, the speed and quality of a second opinion can change everything.

But clarity is only the beginning. Once you have answers, the next question is: now what? That's where the concierge continues to lead — not just identifying the path forward but coordinating every step to get you there faster. From surgery bookings to post-op care, they don't just suggest solutions. They make them happen.

From Answers to Action

When the next step involves surgery, advanced treatment, or cross-border care, speed and precision are no longer optional — they're essential. This is where concierge services shift from insight to execution, transforming diagnostic clarity into timely, coordinated action.

Whether it's accessing private surgery in Canada or arranging specialized treatment abroad, concierge teams manage the entire continuum of care. They schedule procedures, handle pre- and post-operative logistics, coordinate in-home rehab or private nursing, and ensure seamless integration across providers, systems, and even international borders.

In some cases, structural or political limitations within the public system can delay access to urgently needed care. When that happens — and waiting is not an option — going beyond Canada's borders may be the only way forward. It's rarely the preferred route, which is why the next section outlines both domestic and international options. But with growing pressure on the public system, these alternatives have become vital tools in any comprehensive healthcare plan.

What follows is a closer look at how private surgical access and global treatment coordination work — and how they fit into a strategy built for real world complexity, urgency, and results.

Private Surgery: When Time Isn't Optional

In Chapter 5, we explained how provinces allow private surgical clinics to operate legally —the procedures are uninsured, the physicians have opted, and the provincial rules permit billing under those conditions. But knowing these options exist doesn't make them accessible. Not without expert coordination.

This is where concierge support becomes indispensable once again. Because while access may be legal, it's rarely straightforward — and knowing who offers what, under which regulatory framework, is critical to avoiding costly delays or legal missteps.

When surgery becomes the next step — and the public system can't deliver in time — your concierge doesn't just explain your options. They activate them. They know which clinics and boutique hospitals are licensed to operate, which surgeons have opted out of public billing, and where the real windows of availability exist. They also know what isn't possible — and how to work around those limitations, legally and effectively.

This isn't something you can Google. It's strategic, time-sensitive, and precise. From collecting surgical records and verifying diagnostics to securing bookings, managing pre-op consults, handling payment logistics, and organizing post-op rehab — your concierge oversees the entire process.

Case Study: Gallbladder Resolved in Weeks, Not Years

Heidi, 55, Consultant, Pickering - Heidi's gallbladder attacks were becoming more frequent, but her GP quoted a wait time of 12–14 months for surgery. Frustrated and in pain, she turned to a concierge service. Within ten days, she had laparoscopic surgery performed at a Canadian hospital.

In moments like this, private surgery isn't about privilege — it's about momentum. It's what keeps your life, your work, and your health from grinding to a halt. And without a concierge, most of it simply isn't within reach. You could try to navigate it alone — but chances are, you won't know where to start, and the time and money lost in trial and error could cost more than the surgery itself.

Two Paths, One Problem: A Tale of Access

Both Martin and Reena were facing the same issue: a torn rotator cuff that made daily tasks painful and work nearly impossible. Their GPs confirmed surgery was needed. The difference? Martin contacted a concierge service. Reena didn't.

Case Study: Concierge or No Concierge?

Reena was told the wait for a surgical consult would be four months, with surgery following 8 to 10 months after that. She tried to search for private options herself but quickly ran into barriers: unclear regulations, clinics that wouldn't return her calls, and no way to verify if a surgeon was actually available or opted out of the public system. After weeks of trying, she gave up — and resigned herself to waiting.

Martin, on the other hand, contacted his medical concierge the same week he got his diagnosis. Within three days, they had retrieved his imaging, confirmed the need for surgery with a second opinion, and presented him with two available orthopedic specialists at licensed private clinics. Ten days later, Martin had his pre-op consult. Surgery was scheduled within three weeks, followed by a concierge-organized home rehab plan that started within 48 hours of discharge.

Reena waited nearly a year for her care. Martin was back at work within eight weeks. The only difference? Coordination. Knowledge. Access.

When Access Means Everything

Stories like Martin's aren't the exception — they're proof of what's possible when strategy replaces guesswork. Private surgical care in Canada is legal, available, and often life changing — but only if you can navigate the system. That's where concierge teams prove indispensable. They don't just reduce friction; they remove roadblocks.

Still, even the most responsive domestic options have limits. Maybe the procedure you need isn't available in Canada. Maybe the wait times, provincial restrictions, or care caps still leave too much risk on the table. That's when the concierge becomes even more vital — guiding you beyond borders to access world-class medical care, fast. Because when local options fall short, global ones become essential.

When the Map Expands, So Should Your Support

Going global isn't just about finding alternatives — it's about executing them safely, strategically, and without delay. But leaving your home country for medical care can be daunting, especially when surgery is involved — an experience that's already challenging on its own.

At this level, medical advocacy becomes essential. It bridges the gap between complex care and clear, confident decision-making. Whether you're crossing provinces or continents, the stakes are high — and having a trusted partner to coordinate, communicate, and advocate on your behalf isn't just a luxury. It's a necessity.

Medical Advocacy and Case Coordination

Navigating advanced care — especially under pressure — can be overwhelming. That's why many top concierge teams include medical advocates as part of their service.

A medical advocate is your strategic ally. They help interpret complex information, troubleshoot bottlenecks, and support you emotionally and logistically through every step. When you're facing tough decisions or slow-moving systems, they make sure your voice is heard — and your path forward is clear.

Case Study: Beating the Clock with Private Cardiac Care

Elena, age 47, a teacher from Ontario, had been living with increasing fatigue, shortness of breath, and dizzy spells. After weeks of testing, her cardiologist diagnosed her with a faulty heart valve that would eventually require repair. The good news: a minimally invasive valve repair could correct the problem without the trauma of open-heart surgery. The bad news: in Ontario's public system, the wait for the procedure was nearly a year — a dangerous delay for her worsening condition.

Through her concierge team, Elena discovered a private cardiac centre in Quebec that offered the surgery on a self pay basis. The centre's lead surgeon specialized in minimally invasive techniques, allowing for faster recovery, less scarring, and fewer complications.

Her team coordinated everything — the surgical booking, travel arrangements, and a medical advocate to accompany her. In Quebec, the advocate stayed by her side, ensuring she understood every step of the process and that her post-surgery plan was crystal clear before heading home.

Within weeks, Elena's symptoms eased, and she was back to her active life. For her, crossing a provincial border didn't just save time — it protected her health and gave her peace of mind.

When paired with concierge coordination, advocacy shifts from passive to proactive. You're not left waiting, overwhelmed, or uncertain — you're guided with clarity and momentum. And as your care journey becomes more complex, that kind of support becomes not just helpful, but vital.

With advocacy and coordination in place, you're not just prepared to go further — you're positioned to go global. And increasingly, that's where care is headed.

Beyond the Border: Going Global for International Out-of-Country Options

While much of this book focuses on navigating Canada's public and private healthcare systems, there's another strategic pathway that an increasing number of Canadians are pursuing. International care.

For those who move faster than the public system allows — who value speed, precision, and access to advanced treatments — crossing borders is no longer a last resort. It's a proactive, well-informed choice. Whether it's securing a rapid diagnosis, accessing robotic assisted surgery, receiving leading edge cardiac or cancer treatment, or simply obtaining medication not approved domestically, international providers are delivering outcomes that Canada's regulated, waitlist bound system often can't match.

Case Study: Colon Cancer Reimagined in Germany

Marisa, age 58, Interior Designer, Toronto - After being diagnosed with colon cancer, Marisa was told her entire colon would need to be removed — a life altering surgery with major consequences. Unwilling to accept that as her only option, and unable to get a second opinion, she turned to a concierge team for help. Within days, her records were sent to a specialized clinic in Germany. After reviewing her case, the German team proposed a different approach: a targeted injection therapy that could shrink the tumor without removing the colon. She flew to Germany for the first round of treatment. Six weeks later, a follow-up scan in Toronto showed no visible sign of the tumor.

And this isn't underground behavior.

As of 2024, the global medical tourism market was valued at $248.2 billion USD with projected growth to $890.4 billion USD by 2035, according to Future Market Insights February 2025 report, Medical Tourism Market Size, Trends & Forecast 2025–2035. Tens of thousands of Canadians are included in this statistic as they travel abroad each year for medical care, from diagnostics and surgeries to complex therapies and specialist consultations. As delays persist at home, awareness — and demand — continues to rise.

International providers have taken notice. Today, many global medical centers offer streamlined, VIP level experiences with multilingual care teams, highly personalized support, and access to elite specialists in world-class facilities. These aren't just hospitals — they're precision-focused medical hubs where innovation and service are the norm.

But going global comes with complexity. Travel logistics, visa requirements, legal considerations, insurance implications, and post-operative care all need careful coordination. The care may be top-tier — but accessing it effectively requires expertise.

This is another strength of the medical concierge who specializes in international coordination. They manage every layer — from obtaining records and facilitating virtual consults, to scheduling procedures, coordinating physician communication, and ensuring a seamless return to care in Canada. With the right concierge, global care doesn't feel overwhelming. It feels guided.

But international options aren't about escaping the system, it's about designing around its limits. When you factor in lost productivity, delayed outcomes, personal stress, and the cumulative cost of waiting, going global for care is often the best solution. It's efficient and intentional, and in many cases, it's the most important decision you'll ever make to protect your health.

But with that capability comes a new kind of responsibility because none of this can happen passively.

The Second Floor Is Built — But It Doesn't Come for Free

The second floor of your healthcare strategy isn't theoretical. It's real. It's available. And in a growing number of cases, it's the only thing standing between timely recovery and irreversible decline.

But here's the part most people overlook until it's too late: this level of care isn't publicly funded. It's not automatically available. And it doesn't arrive just because you need it.

That's why access to this tier must be treated as essential — not as a luxury, a last resort, or a conversation for later because far too many Canadians are already arriving at this level without warning, without guidance, without planning, and without the ability to act.

Whether or not someone chooses to pursue private care is a personal decision. But either way, they deserve to know their options in advance — what's available, where to find it, and how to act on it — long before it becomes urgent.

From a professional perspective, this is the foundation of modern healthcare planning — and what sets it apart from the traditional approach. Conventional planning models focus exclusively on income replacement or expense reimbursement, ignoring the actual mechanics of access and the risk associated with it. But if care is delayed, what exactly are you protecting? Modern access planning starts with the premise that true protection means anticipating the possibility of funding care yourself — and putting a plan in place so that, if the need arises, treatment can happen without delay.

Access without funding isn't access at all. And when the public system can't provide what's needed in time, the only path forward is private — which means the cost becomes personal. Whether it's covered by an individual, an employer, or a private insurer, that cost is real. And the risk of not planning for it is even more real.

That brings us to Chapter 8.

There, we'll break down the numbers — from what you're already paying into the public system to what private care actually costs — so you can prepare with clarity, not react in crisis.

Because protection isn't just about having a plan. It's about knowing what that strategy requires — and whether you're truly ready to fund it.

Chapter 8

The True Cost of Control

So far, we've explored the structure of a modern healthcare plan — from the overburdened public foundation to the private services that restore access when timing matters most. We've reviewed the products and services designed to help you navigate delays and examined their limitations.

But one critical piece remains: what does this level of control actually cost?

Whether it's a concierge membership, advanced diagnostics, out-of-country surgery, or rapid access to specialists, these options aren't pre-funded. There's no tax refund, no reimbursement. If you want them — you pay.

So, whether you're planning for yourself or advising clients, a complete strategy with this in mind requires financial clarity. In this chapter, we'll break down the numbers — what you're already contributing, what private options demand, and just how fast the costs can escalate when time, health, or income is at risk.

The Hidden Costs of Public Care

One of the most persistent and comforting myths in Canada is the idea that our healthcare is free.

We hear it from politicians, we repeat it in casual conversation, and we take pride in it as a defining feature of Canadian identity. For many, it's almost sacred — a symbol of fairness, compassion, and equality. And on the surface, it's easy to believe because you can walk into a clinic, get seen, and walk out without paying a bill.

You may already know the system isn't truly free — but have you ever looked closely at what it really costs, and how it's funded?

Since we're talking about numbers in this chapter — and laying the groundwork for comparing public and private solutions — this is the right moment to clarify what you're already paying. Because when you do the math, the idea of free quickly collapses.

The truth is simple but uncomfortable: healthcare in Canada isn't free. It's prepaid.

Every year, all taxpaying Canadians fund our healthcare system through a web of income taxes, corporate taxes, and provincial levies — whether you use it or not. And yet, when you need it, you're often met with waitlists, unavailable specialists, and administrative dead ends.

You're not just paying into the system - you're subsidizing it - and for anyone in a higher tax bracket the cost is far greater than most people realize. Due to the structure of the funding and the tax burden, it becomes clear: the public system is expensive — and yet, in many cases, incomplete.

How the Public System is Funded

Let's take a moment to break down where the money for Canada's public healthcare system actually comes from — and why that matters when planning for what the system can't provide.

At the national level, the primary funding mechanism is the Canada Health Transfer (CHT). This is how the federal government supports provincial and territorial healthcare systems. Every year, billions of dollars flow from Ottawa to the provinces through this program, which is funded by federal income taxes, corporate taxes, and other general revenues. Importantly, these transfers are distributed on a per-capita basis — meaning each province receives funding based solely on its population size, not on the severity of local wait times, the complexity of care required, or the volume of need.

From there, the responsibility shifts to the provinces and territories — where healthcare is actually delivered. They manage hospitals, control waitlists, regulate services, and fund a large portion of healthcare costs on their own. This is done through a mix of personal and corporate income taxes, sales taxes (like PST or HST), and, in some cases, health premiums or levies. For example, both Ontario and British Columbia have had versions of these, though many are now being restructured or absorbed into general revenues.

Over time, these costs have become less transparent to the average Canadian. In the past, some provinces issued clear annual statements labeled as health premiums — giving people a concrete sense of what they were paying. But even though the itemization was phased out, the financial burden didn't go away. It was simply folded into broader taxation, making it harder for individuals to understand what they're actually contributing — and what they're getting in return.

What You're Really Paying

According to the Fraser Institute's 2024 report, a typical Canadian family pays between $7,000 and $15,000 annually in healthcare related taxes, depending on income. For higher earning households — especially dual-income professionals — that number can climb past $40,000 a year.

These aren't marginal contributions. They're substantial investments — made regardless of whether you receive timely care or not. And that's the paradox: you fund a public system that often can't deliver, then pay again when you're forced to go private. It's not just inefficient. It's financially disorienting.

Let's be honest — these numbers are hard to swallow. It's no wonder so many Canadians cling to the idea that our healthcare system is working as intended. The truth is painful: we're spending tens of thousands of dollars a year on a promise that often goes unfulfilled. And when the system fails to deliver, the emotional frustration is compounded by financial disbelief. It's easier not to think about it.

But this isn't about blame — and it's certainly not about giving up. It's about being informed. Yes, in a perfect world, we'd receive the money ourselves and choose how to allocate it — to public care, private services, or a blend of both. But that's not the system we have. So, we have to work within the one we've got. And whether you're an average Canadian trying to plan ahead or a professional advising others, that starts with knowing the facts.

Because painful as this may be to read, it's important. It's the kind of understanding that empowers better decisions — not just in personal planning, but in public conversation. The next time we go to vote, maybe we remember this. Maybe we ask better questions. Maybe we insist that healthcare reform — real reform — is finally on the table.

Whatever your politics, the numbers matter. Because they're already affecting your life, whether you realize it or not. So now that we've looked at what you're already paying into the system, let's look at the other side of the equation.

What Would It Cost to Get What You Actually Need?

By now, you've probably come to terms with the fact that public healthcare in Canada isn't truly free. Here's the next uncomfortable truth: private care isn't cheap. But given the state of the system today, it's often the only reliable path to timely access, clear answers, and a sense of control.

And yet, when you're already contributing tens of thousands in taxes each year, the idea of paying even more out-of-pocket can feel unfair — even infuriating. But this is the reality we're working with. The costs are real. And if you're serious about securing faster, more personalized care, you need to know what it looks like before you can make informed decisions — or build a plan that actually works.

This isn't about fear. It's about financial clarity. Let's look at the numbers.

Private Care: Real Costs, Real Considerations

So, what does private care really cost?

Below are real examples from Canadian and international providers. While costs vary by clinic and geography, the goal here isn't to pin down exact pricing — it's to give you a practical sense of the financial landscape.

Whether you're planning for yourself, a loved one, or a client, these numbers offer a clearer view of what's required when waiting is no longer an option.

Private Clinic Memberships: Not all memberships are created equal, but most fall within a similar range. Currently, an annual membership at a leading Canadian wellness provider costs around $3,885 for adults, and $3,110 for children. This includes access to uninsured services only via a dedicated physician, with same or next day appointments, after-hour nursing support, a care co-ordination team, and prescription delivery. More robust services

— such as executive assessments, wellness packages or enhanced screening — increase cost from the base plan, with some offering comprehensive packages for over $10,900 per year, per person, plus tax.

Health Assessments: Top tier clinics offer standalone health assessments for various reasons and rates from $1500 to more than $5000. These typically include additional screening tests with same-day results — but the service stops at the assessment. Follow-up care, if needed, is billed separately or referred out.

Diagnostic Imaging: Private imaging offers speed — but it comes at a cost. In Canada, a single body part MRI typically ranges from $400 to $1,500, depending on the type of scan and location. Full-body MRI scans are more expensive, generally running from $1,500 to $3,250, with some specialized providers listing prices up to $3,500. These fees usually exclude interpretation, physician consultations, and referrals.

Nurse Practitioner Services: Private nurse practitioners charge $65 to over $120 per hour, depending on location and credentials. In Toronto, many top tier professionals charge around $90/hour. These services are typically paid out of pocket and are frequently used within medical concierge programs.

Domestic Surgical Procedures: Estimates for privately paid knee replacement surgery in Canada generally fall between $20,000 and $30,000 CAD, according to Timely Medical, HQ Ontario, and the Canadian Journal of Surgery. For example, Ortho Westmount, a private orthopedic clinic in Quebec, lists the cost of a total knee arthroplasty at $21,000 CAD and knee arthroplasty at $21,500 CAD — figures that align with the national range.

Spinal and Neurological Surgery: Private spinal procedures in Canada can be costly, and prices vary significantly by province. In Alberta and British Columbia, where some surgeons have opted out of the public billing system or work within private surgical centers, complex procedures such as spinal fusion can range from $40,000 to over $110,000, depending on the number of levels fused and the facility. In Quebec, private clinics may offer certain spine surgeries at lower rates, but even then, costs typically start around $25,000 for less complex cases.

Domestic Cardiac Care: Exact pricing for expedited cardiac surgery in Canada is not widely published, but RCM Health Consultancy reports that procedures coordinated through private Canadian facilities can range from $20,000 to $50,000, depending on the complexity and location.

International Cardiac Care: In the U.S., out-of-pocket prices for coronary artery bypass grafting (CABG) vary widely. Debt.org reports that open heart bypass surgery can range from $30,000 to over $200,000 USD, depending on hospital type, geographic location, and surgical complexity. Additionally, the average price in Florida hovers around $57,125 USD, covering surgeon and facility fees but excluding travel, lodging, and rehabilitation costs.

As you can see, the costs are steep — but the value lies in what you gain: time, clarity, control, and in some cases, survival. This is why planning matters. These aren't surprise expenses. They're foreseeable, and they deserve a place in any comprehensive healthcare strategy. You may not be able to control when you'll need care — or how the public system will respond — but you can control whether you're financially prepared to act if private care becomes your only option. Because in healthcare, few things are more expensive than waiting too long to act.

These aren't hypothetical numbers. Let's look at two real-life scenarios that show how quickly private costs can escalate — and why financial preparation is critical.

Case Study 1: When Time is the Problem

Mark, 52 — Automotive Executive, Toronto: Mark is a busy executive running a luxury car dealership in Toronto. He's sharp, driven, and constantly on — balancing a demanding business and an active family life. But when he suddenly develops intense nerve pain radiating from his neck to his right arm, everything changes. Within days, the pain becomes so severe he can't even hold a phone to his ear.

He can't concentrate. He can't take client calls. It hurts to drive and send emails.

After weeks of hoping it will go away, he finally sees his GP, who orders an MRI and refers him to a neurologist. But the first available specialist appointment is 6–9 months away, and the MRI is at least three months out. Meanwhile, his doctor tells him to rest to avoid making it worse. He needs to work, so that's impossible, but he limits any travel and tries to work from home. He's stressed out and miserable from the helplessness.

The pressure mounts until eventually another month later Mark does what many professionals in his position are forced to do: he looks for the private option. He pays for a medical concierge to coordinate faster diagnostics, spending $1,200 for an MRI. After they get the results he flies out of the country for a spinal surgery — a discectomy and nerve decompression — at a specialized U.S. clinic. The total? Nearly $100,000, including surgery, travel, accommodations, and post-op care. All of it paid out of pocket.

Case Study 2: When Coverage Falls Short

Danielle, 49 — Interior Designer, Toronto: Mark's wife, Danielle, runs her own boutique interior design business . When she begins experiencing sharp abdominal pain, her doctor is concerned and sends her for an ultrasound. While she waits for results her life is disrupted. Then she gets a call and is referred to a gynecologist — but the wait is three months long. In the meantime, she's told to rest and avoid stress. But as a business owner and the mother of two teenagers, downtime isn't an option.

The emotional toll grows. She can't manage client projects. She can't sleep. She can't function — but she also can't get answers, and this is the worst part.

After almost two months of waiting for a cancelation, she turns to a medical concierge. Faster diagnostics lead to a surgical recommendation — but the wait in Ontario is six months or more. Hoping to avoid the private cost, she waits a few more months, but the symptoms continue to escalate. Eventually, Danielle accepts that she needs to go abroad and travels to Baltimore for surgery.

The total cost — including expedited consultations, international surgery, travel for four, recovery time, and Mark's time away from work — exceeds $60,000. Again: all of it out of pocket. All of it unplanned.

These two stories aren't rare exceptions — they're examples of a broader, systemic problem. They reveal what happens when real people run headfirst into real delays, and just how quickly the costs can spiral when the public system can't respond in time. Whether it's the primary earner or a dependent, the outcome is often the same: a scramble to fund urgent care that should've been accessible — but wasn't.

The Bottom Line

Control over your healthcare is powerful — but it comes at a price. You fund the public system through taxes, and then, when that system fails to deliver, you pay again — out of pocket, often under pressure, and without warning.

The impact isn't just inefficient. It's destabilizing. It can threaten your health, your financial security, your business continuity, and your peace of mind.

These aren't hypothetical risks. Every day, thousands of Canadians face the same choice: wait months for care or pay tens of thousands in private fees.

This is why a modern, integrated healthcare strategy is essential. It's the final layer of your structure — the roof — and the most important part. Designed to proactively protect everything beneath it, the right plan absorbs financial shocks and prevents instability when you have no other option. Because when the storm hits, it's not just your health at stake — it's everything you've built.

In Chapter 10, we'll walk through how to build this kind of comprehensive plan — one that connects access, funding, and planning into a single, resilient system.

But first, there's one emerging solution you need to know about — a product that's quietly transforming what's possible in Canadian healthcare planning: international medical insurance. Few people even know it exists, yet it's bridging the very gap we've just uncovered. That's where we're headed next.

Chapter 9

The Game Changer: International Medical Insurance

You've seen the gap. You understand the risks. You've reviewed the costs — and the reality that control doesn't come cheap.

So now the question becomes: if the public system can't meet your needs — and Canadian private care is often restricted by law or difficult to access — how do you secure timely treatment without bearing the full financial burden alone?

That's where international medical insurance (IMI) comes in.

Still relatively new to the Canadian market, IMI is quietly filling one of the biggest voids in our healthcare system: it provides insured coverage for medically necessary treatment outside the country when timely care isn't available at home. In doing so, it bridges the two most urgent challenges we've discussed — access and funding.

It transforms what is usually a high-cost, high-stress scramble into a structured, insured solution — one that restores control, preserves capital, and protects your health when the stakes are high.

In this chapter, we'll walk through how it works, what it covers (and what it doesn't), when it applies, and why so few Canadians — including professional planners, consultants and insurance advisors — are not even aware it exists. We'll also clear up common misconceptions and explain why this isn't just another product, but a critical evolution in modern healthcare planning.

Understanding the Role of Private Insurance in Canada

Across the developed world, most countries operate with a mix of public and private healthcare. Some lean heavily on private models, while others blend the two. Although structures vary, two key facts remain consistent: both public and private systems offer the same core medical services, and access to private care is funded through insurance.

Canada is unique in relying exclusively on a public healthcare system, with private providers legally prohibited from duplicating its core functions. Yet contrary to popular belief, private healthcare does exist — it actually predates the universal model and continues to grow in response to demand. The crucial distinction is that, in Canada, anyone seeking private care must cover the full cost out of pocket. Under the Canada Health Act, private insurance cannot reimburse for treatments already covered publicly, effectively eliminating the possibility of a parallel market.

This legal restriction is the foundation for the product we're exploring in this chapter. While it's called International Medical Insurance, the Canadian version isn't a carbon copy of what's sold abroad. Instead, it's been redesigned and adapted into a hybrid model that operates fully within the legal boundaries of the Canada Health Act.

The key difference is where the coverage applies. The policy is structured to fund treatment outside of Canada — including surgeries and specialist care — so it never competes directly with provincially insured services performed domestically. In other words, it bypasses waitlists by moving care abroad, where the Act's billing restrictions don't apply.

That said, there are limited situations where this coverage can also be used for domestic private care. This includes services that are not covered by the public plan, procedures performed by physicians who have opted out of the public system, or surgeries in licensed private facilities operating outside provincial billing streams. In rare cases, policies may also cover treatment in a Canadian private facility if it qualifies under a nearest suitable facility provision — typically for urgent or specialized care.

Because it's fundamentally an insurance product, it's also offered in strategic partnership with a licensed Canadian insurer, ensuring full compliance with the Insurance Companies Act and other regulatory requirements.

Now that you understand how this product fits within the legal framework, the next question is: what does it actually include? While it doesn't include primary care or core services, it still offers powerful combination of benefits designed to ensure timely access to treatment when it's needed most. Let's take a closer look at what this coverage provides, how it works in practice, and why it's such a critical component of modern healthcare planning.

What Is Included

As a specialized solution, the Canadian version of this product is designed to organize and fund medically necessary surgery or treatment following a diagnosed illness or injury. Unlike traditional insurance policies that pay the policyholder directly for income loss or expense reimbursement, this coverage pays the healthcare provider directly on the policyholders behalf to ensure immediate access to care without financial roadblocks.

Once a diagnosis is received, right or wrong, the policy can be activated. Treatment is received at centers of excellence, private clinics, hospitals, or specialty providers, with no geographic restrictions. The care follows the need — not the borders. Coverage begins with a deductible, selected at the time of setup and beyond that, annual maximums range from $1 to $5 million.

In addition, every policy includes access to a dedicated medical concierge — a professional team that manages all the logistics, and there is a variety of other enhancements that can be added on the base depending on how its set up.

Together, these features form a powerful support system — one that's designed not only to deliver care, but to remove the barriers that so often delay it. But beyond the individual benefits, this product holds broader significance in the evolving landscape of Canadian healthcare.

Why Is This Product Significant

This model is designed to address two of the most pressing challenges in Canadian healthcare today: securing timely access and providing reliable funding.

While it doesn't cover primary care, it zeroes in on what matters most. Recalling our house metaphor, the ground floor represents routine and preventative care, while the upper level includes concierge support and advanced, time-sensitive, often life-saving treatment. This product is focused squarely on that second floor. And as we explored in the chapter on cost, these are the services that are both the most expensive, the hardest to avoid, and the ones with the longest wait time. So, it's here—where delays are dangerous and out-of-pocket costs can be overwhelming—that this solution offers the greatest value.

Also, beyond its practical benefits, the existence of this product signals something bigger: change. Though it operates entirely within the guidelines of the Act, its presence in the market reflects a growing willingness to innovate. Similar to the gradual expansion of provincial drug plans, which began as targeted initiatives and have evolved in response to need, this policy reflects a first step toward addressing an overlooked gap in the healthcare system.

But despite its potential to drive meaningful change, this policy remains largely under the radar. If it signals the beginning of a shift in how Canadians can access care, it begs a deeper question: what difference does it actually make when someone has this coverage — and when they don't?

To illustrate, let's walk through a real-world comparison.

Case Study: Two Paths, One Diagnosis

David, a 47-year-old business owner from Toronto, begins experiencing severe back pain and mobility issues. After navigating a long wait for diagnostic imaging and a specialist consult through the public system, he receives a diagnosis: spinal stenosis. The surgeon recommends monitoring the condition but offers no timeline for reassessment or intervention. David disagrees with the recommendation. He feels his symptoms are worsening and wants to act — but he's stuck. He can't get another referral, and the system offers no clear path forward.

Now let's look at what happens next — first without coverage, and then with international medical insurance in place.

Without coverage, David decides to take matters into his own hands. He pays out of pocket for a private healthcare concierge to help coordinate a second opinion and arrange care outside of Canada. The process is stressful and expensive. He spends thousands just getting reassessed, and ultimately books surgery at a reputable clinic in the U.S. The total bill for surgery, diagnostics, travel, and post-operative care exceeds $60,000 — and none of it is covered by insurance. While the care is excellent and timely, David bears the full financial and logistical burden, all while managing his recovery.

Now imagine the same scenario — but this time, David has international medical insurance. Upon receiving the initial diagnosis, he makes a claim. Within weeks, the insurance provider arranges a full reassessment, including new diagnostics and expert consultations. The concierge team identifies a partner facility across the U.S. border that specializes in his condition, schedules the procedure promptly, and coordinates every detail from start to finish. David pays his $2,500 deductible on top of his annual premium $1,608. Both expenses are run through his health spending account, making them fully tax-deductible. Aside from those costs, there's no significant financial burden — and no time lost trying to manage the system alone.

The care he receives is the same. The difference is how he gets there.

Without insurance, David spends weeks scrambling and over $60,000 out of pocket. With insurance, he's treated promptly, supported every step of the way, and pays a fraction of the cost — for a better overall experience. This isn't just about funding. It's about access, advocacy, and control. And in moments like this, those things make all the difference.

Stories like David's raise an important question: if this kind of coverage can offer such a dramatic improvement in outcome, why don't more people know it exists? That brings us to one of the biggest challenges this product faces — awareness.

Understanding the Awareness Gap

Private medical insurance is still relatively new to the Canadian market — not because the need didn't exist, but because demand is only now catching up. Public system delays and growing wait times have created space for innovation, and international providers are beginning to meet that need.

Yet most Canadians are still unaware — and that's not their fault. We've been conditioned to believe there are only two options: wait and hope or pay out of pocket and pray it's affordable. To make matters worse, many still assume private care is either illegal or reserved for the ultra-wealthy. Of course, neither of these assumptions is true — but this mindset means few people go searching for alternatives until a crisis forces them to do so.

And it's not just consumers who are in the dark. There's also a combination of systemic limitations and professional blind spots that hinder awareness.

Ideology remains a major barrier. Even among professionals who are aware of the product, many are influenced by long-standing beliefs about how Canadian healthcare works. They often assume that private or international options are either unnecessary or unavailable. This mindset, shaped by the same cultural conditioning that affects consumers, leads them to default to familiar offerings—life, disability, critical illness, and group benefits—because these are easier to explain, widely accepted, and don't challenge the public healthcare narrative. Without a strong ideological shift, many advisors simply avoid recommending what they don't fully understand or believe in.

Education is another critical factor. Most advisors have not been trained as Certified Healthcare Access Planners™, and as a result, they lack the framework needed to assess healthcare-related risks and position international medical insurance within a comprehensive strategy. Without this specialized knowledge, they struggle to present innovative, healthcare-specific solutions with clarity and confidence—leaving clients without the informed guidance they increasingly need to navigate a public system that no longer guarantees timely access to care.

This lack of awareness — both among consumers and advisors — has allowed several persistent myths to take hold. These misconceptions not only prevent people from exploring their options, but also reinforce the belief that timely, private care is either out of reach or out of bounds. Before we go any further, let's take a moment to debunk the most common misunderstandings about what this coverage is, how it works, and who it's really for.

Myth #1: Group Benefits Include This Coverage

One of the most common misconceptions is that this type of coverage is already included in employee benefit plans. While it's true that you can buy this coverage corporately, the reality is that the product is still relatively new to the Canadian market, and for many reasons as already mentioned, its not mainstream yet. So, for now, anyone assuming it's already part of their benefits package is likely mistaken.

It's an understandable assumption however — especially for professionals with comprehensive plans. But in truth, most group plans out there fall into the standard category of supplemental coverage. They're designed to reimburse routine expenses or provide income protection, not to deliver immediate access to private medical treatment in the midst of a serious health crisis.

This misunderstanding around benefits is just one part of a larger pattern — where lack of awareness breeds assumptions. And perhaps the most common assumption of all? That this kind of coverage must be unaffordable.

Myth #2: There's No Way I Can Afford It

For all the reasons outlined in this book, it's no surprise that when Canadians first learn about this product the immediate reaction is always the same: first, they question whether it's legal; then, they assume it must be an elite product reserved for the ultra-wealthy.

And to be fair, that assumption makes sense. We're talking about private hospitals, accelerated diagnostics, top-tier specialists, international treatment coordination, and concierge-level service — all of which *sound* like the domain of high-net-worth individuals.

But here's the surprising truth — and something we can all relate to, especially in an era of soaring auto theft: in many cases, the annual premium for private international medical insurance is about the same as, or even less than, what most Canadians already pay to insure their car.

That may sound counterintuitive, but it actually makes perfect sense when you understand how insurance works. Premiums aren't arbitrary — they're based on actuarial science, using large-scale data to predict risk across age groups, deductibles, and coverage limits. It's not guess-work. It's risk pooling — and when done properly, it makes comprehensive, high-value protection financially accessible to the average policyholder.

So, the reality is, this isn't an elite or luxury benefit for the top one percent — it's a practical, actuarially priced option for Canadians who can't afford to wait months for care or absorb six-figure treatment costs out of pocket.

Completing the Structure

As we close this chapter, I hope you now see why international medical insurance deserves a place in the conversation — and in many cases, a place in your plan. Like every tool we've explored, it has pros and cons. But it's the only solution that directly addresses both access and funding — two of the biggest gaps in Canadian healthcare today.

The reality is, we don't have endless options. That's why planning in Canada requires a different mindset: strategic, informed, and sometimes creative.

We've established that coverage without access is meaningless, access without funding is impossible, and funding without planning is reckless. This is exactly why healthcare delays are a real risk — and why your structure isn't finished until you've added the final protective layer: the roof.

That roof is the deliberate, forward-thinking strategy — the system that protects everything beneath it: your health, your income, your time, your future. Without it, even the strongest foundation is exposed. And when the storm hits, it's too late to start building.

In Chapter 10, we shift from understanding to action. You'll learn how to bring all the pieces together into a resilient, layered plan — one that goes beyond individual products to form a cohesive system of protection. We'll explore how to build it, what to include, and why expert guidance can make the difference between a fragile idea and a fully protected future.

Chapter 10

Designing Your Healthcare Access Plan

At this point in the book, you've done more than learn — you've unlearned.

You've moved past the assumptions most Canadians carry about healthcare: that public care is always available, that private options are illegal, and that planning begins and ends with income protection. You now understand that the real risk isn't just getting sick — it's not being able to access treatment in time.

Now it's time to build a plan that reflects that reality.

In this chapter, we move from awareness to action — from scattered products to a unified strategy. We'll walk through the key components of a modern healthcare access plan and explain how each layer contributes to a system that protects your health, your finances, your time, and your independence.

Whether you're building a plan for yourself, your family, or your business, the goal is the same: to create a structure that holds up when everything else feels uncertain. A structure that's not just reactive, but resilient — and built for the world we live in today.

The Four Tiers of Healthcare Access in Canada

What follows is a summary of the core layers we've explored throughout this book — a practical overview to help you visualize your next steps.

Level 1: Public Healthcare

At the foundation is the public healthcare system — the layer most Canadians rely on for nearly everything: hospital access, emergency services, primary care, referrals, requisitions, and diagnostics. It's built for the population, not the individual. Reactive, not proactive. The major issues include long wait times, system overload, and inconsistent coverage across provinces. It's where care begins, but not where it should end.

Level 2: Private Preventative Care

This next layer consists of private, routine care: specialty clinics, diagnostics, telehealth, and other preventative services not covered by the public system. These services are more proactive and accessible — for those who can afford them — but vary significantly in cost and availability by province. However, they remain transactional in nature and often refer patients back to the public system for anything beyond basic care.

Level 3: Healthcare Navigation & Coordination

This layer adds coordination and strategy. Concierge healthcare services help navigate the system, manage referrals, connect diagnostics to treatment, facilitate second opinions, and organize access to advanced care — both domestically and internationally. It's the difference between having information and having a plan. As with the previous layer, options and affordability usually vary by region.

Level 4: Advanced and International Treatment

At the top tier is access to private surgical clinics, advanced therapies, innovative technologies, breakthrough medications, and high-quality recovery and post-operative care — both in Canada and abroad. This is where speed and precision matter most. The main barrier here is cost, as this level of care typically requires significant out-of-pocket investment.

This is the high ground — but it's not automatic. Accessing this level of care requires planning, foresight, and a clear strategy. Now that we've reviewed what's available, it's time to focus on what's essential: building a healthcare plan that works for you. Let's move from services to structure.

Assembling Your Strategy

From a professional consulting perspective, this is where the real work begins. Not with products or policies, but with questions. Because no two people are alike. Your age, health history, family structure, income model, business setup, travel patterns, and even your comfort with uncertainty all shape how your healthcare strategy should be designed.

Healthcare planning doesn't exist in isolation. It intersects with financial planning, tax efficiency, risk management — and in most cases, investment strategy. That's why generic advice falls short, and why there's no way to prescribe a universal formula that everyone reading this book can use. What we can offer is a framework for smart, strategic decision-making.

Here are six steps to help you start shaping a plan that fits your life:

Step 1: Review What You Already Have

Start with a clear and thorough audit of your current healthcare coverage. What public services do you rely on? What group or private insurance policies are in place? Do you have any supplemental benefits — and if so, what exactly do they cover? Consider your current health concerns and needs, and examine each plan for limitations, exclusions, or gaps you may have overlooked.

But your review shouldn't stop at healthcare coverage. To build a truly effective strategy, you need to see the full picture. That means taking stock of any relevant financial tools and plans already in place — including life, disability, international medical and critical illness insurance, as well as retirement savings, education funds, emergency reserves, and estate plans. Understanding these elements helps you see what resources you have to work with, what overlaps, where the conflicts are, and what needs to be restructured.

This step is critical because it reveals where you're protected — and where you're exposed. You can't move forward with confidence until you understand your starting point.

Step 2: Define What You Need or Value Most

Go beyond anticipating potential medical events — this step is about identifying what truly matters to you. Is it speed of primary care, flexible access, convenience, peace of mind, or maintaining control during a crisis? Consider your role: are you the primary income earner? Do you travel frequently? Would delays in care threaten your business, career, or family stability? Who depends on you — and who or what do you depend on?

Clarifying these personal and practical priorities helps ensure your healthcare strategy is tailored to your real world risks and responsibilities — not just generic coverage needs.

Step 3: Identify the Gaps Between the Two

This is where most blind spots tend to surface. The healthcare layer you're currently operating within may not align with what you value most — whether that's speed, control, access, or peace of mind. Many people assume they're protected, until they discover they're not.

Gaps often appear in areas like diagnostics, wait times for surgery, specialist access, or continuity of care. But they also emerge when you compare your insured protection strategy (life, disability, critical illness, international medical insurance) to your actual priorities and responsibilities. You may begin to realize that what's in place doesn't reflect what matters most — or what's truly at risk.

This step is crucial because identifying the disconnect between what you have, want and need is the only way to build a meaningful, effective plan. Without this clarity, you're operating on assumptions — and in any form of planning, especially healthcare, assumptions can be costly. If you skip this step, there's no way to accurately pinpoint the gaps, which means there's no way to find or implement the right solutions to fill them.

Step 4: Explore Targeted Solutions to Fill the Gaps

Once you've identified what's missing, the next step is to explore the solutions available to address those needs. This might include the purchase of a international medical insurance policy, a basic membership with a concierge, connection with an advanced diagnostic clinic, the addition of a specialty practitioner for annual performance physicals, or an individual benefit plan with a high medication limit. The key is aligning the right tool with the right risk — and building a strategy that evolves as your life, work, health, or family circumstances change.

There's no one-size-fits-all answer here. The right solution depends entirely on your unique situation — what you value, what you need, want, and what you already have. That's why this step offers such a wide range of options. Because if you don't know what's available, you're working with incomplete information — and you can't build a strong plan without all the pieces. Decisions require knowledge, and in healthcare planning, knowledge truly is power. Without it, you may overlook critical solutions, miss opportunities to protect yourself or your family, and end up defaulting to a system that guarantees long delays when it matters most.

Throughout this book, we've outlined the most current products and services available to Canadians today — but this landscape will continue to evolve. New options will emerge as the industry responds to rising demand and changing expectations. Staying informed is what keeps your strategy effective and future-ready.

Step 5: Reassess Your Costs and Coverage with Strategy in Mind

Many clients are surprised to discover they're overpaying for the wrong protection — covered for things they rarely use, while lacking coverage in the areas where they're most vulnerable. This misalignment often stems from outdated policies, planning for the wrong risk, reliance on default employer plans, or assumptions that haven't been revisited in years.

This step is critical because your resources are not unlimited. Most people can't afford every option available — and they shouldn't have to. That's why the previous steps are so important: by clarifying what you have, what you value, and where the gaps lie, you're now in a position to allocate your funds more efficiently and purposefully.

Based on everything we've reviewed in this book, this step is especially important if you're restructuring an existing plan — because you're now working from a modern approach that recognizes delays in healthcare access as a primary and evolving risk.

A well aligned, rebalanced plan can reduce unnecessary costs, eliminate redundancies, and sharpen your focus on what truly matters. It ensures that every dollar you invest in protection is working toward your specific goals — not merely expanding a generic template. This kind of strategy takes careful consideration of all the moving parts, but only then can you arrive at a strong, streamlined structure that reflects both your budget and your actual needs.

Step 6: Decide If You're Building Solo — or With a Specialist

Be honest — are you feeling overwhelmed yet?

If so, you're not alone. The steps above involve a lot to consider insurance, finances, healthcare systems, personal values, evolving risks — and that's before you factor in life changes, family needs, or business responsibilities. Even with a strong framework in hand, this is the point where many people hesitate. The decisions are complex, the stakes are high, and your time and energy are already spread thin.

A proper review requires more than just good intentions. It takes industry knowledge, tax fluency, product understanding, and the ability to balance protection with affordability — all while anticipating future needs. That's why many people choose not to go it alone. Instead, they work with someone who does this every day — someone who knows where to look, what questions to ask, and how to turn insights into action.

If you're working with a Certified Healthcare Access Planner™, you're already a step ahead. These specialists are trained specifically to bring all of these components together — healthcare, insurance, strategy, and planning — into one clear, actionable path. Their role is to help you cut through the complexity, avoid costly mistakes, and move forward with clarity and confidence.

But whether you build solo, or with support, the goal remains the same: a healthcare strategy that works when you need it most — because in today's system, this is no longer something you can leave to chance.

Now that we've walked through the six foundational steps to building a modern healthcare strategy, it's time to see how these principles come to life in the real world. The following case studies illustrate how different clients applied this framework based on their unique needs, values, and circumstances.

Case Study: Two Outcomes, One Choice

Pietro is a 52-year-old marketing consultant and small business owner. Recently divorced with one adult child who lives overseas, he decided to launch his own consultancy after being packaged out of a corporate role he held for 23 years. His income is modest at $75,000, but sales are good, and most of his capital has been reinvested into building the business. He employs a small team but has no active group benefits in place.

Like many professionals, Pietro assumed he was adequately protected with a combination of public healthcare and personal insurance. He pays $650/month for two individual policies: a $100,000 critical illness plan and a long-term disability policy with additional riders. His savings are limited due to the divorce, with most of his resources tied up in the business. He prefers using public healthcare for routine needs, but if something serious were to happen, he values speed, clarity, and the ability to act quickly to avoid downtime.

That moment arrives when Pietro begins experiencing chest discomfort and shortness of breath. It's subtle at first

— just enough to raise concern but not alarming enough for the emergency room. What happens next depends entirely on the strategy he has in place.

Strategy A: Reactive by Default

Pietro books an appointment with his family doctor — the earliest availability is in a week. Although he considers visiting a walk-in clinic, he decides to wait, preferring the continuity of care from his regular physician.

At the appointment, his doctor orders diagnostic tests. It takes another 10 business days to get them done. The results are completed but sit for four more days. When his doctor finally reviews them, she refers him to a cardiologist — with a wait time of two to four months.

In the meantime, his symptoms worsen. He cancels meetings, delays travel and struggles to concentrate. Eventually, the situation escalates, and he goes to the ER. There, after a ten hour wait, he see's a cardiologist, who confirms a procedure is needed — necessary, but not urgent — placing him on yet another waitlist with medication.

Despite paying $650/month for a long-term disability policy and a critical illness plan, neither policy pays out. With no group benefits, limited liquidity, and no access strategy in place, his income stops if he doesn't work. He begins paying out-of-pocket for medication and considers dipping into his RRSP to get the procedure done privately but lacks guidance or clarity.

The result: more than six months of uncertainty, financial pressure, and emotional strain. No income. No direction. No support. The real cost is more than financial — it's disruption to health, business, and peace of mind.

Now let's rewind and imagine a different path.

Strategy B: Proactive by Design

Referred by a colleague, Pietro engages a Certified Healthcare Access Planner™ to review his healthcare and insurance setup. The planner identifies that while Pietro is comfortable using public care for routine services, he wants and needs clarity, speed and more options for anything more advanced — all while working within the financial constraints of a growing business.

They restructure his plan accordingly. A small group benefits package is set up through the business, including unlimited drug coverage, short and long term disability, telemedicine, and a health spending account (HSA). Costs are shared with his team, tax-deductible, and require no personal outlay.

His individual disability policy is adjusted — the benefit is reduced to act as a top-up to group coverage, unnecessary riders are removed, and the premium is paid through the business. His critical illness policy is cancelled. In its place, he purchases international medical insurance for $2,575/year that's reimbursed through the HSA and a concierge membership for $500/year paid for by the corporation.

Pietro continues using his GP for routine care, but now has advanced, private options available when speed and coordination matter most.

When delays arise with his GP, he uses his telemedicine benefit to receive a same-day requisition. When told diagnostics will take 10 days, he contacts the concierge, who arranges private testing within 72 hours. The results are reviewed the next day, confirming the need for a non-urgent procedure. As he has a diagnosis, the concierge team coordinates with the international medical insurer, who provide the care of the procedure in full. He pays his $2500 deductible, (which he then claims through his HSA), and three weeks from first symptom Pietro is recovering.

Your Next Step: From Insight to Implementation

Both scenarios began the same way — with a few troubling symptoms. But the outcomes were determined entirely by the strategy that was (or wasn't) in place before the crisis began.

The contrast between reactive and proactive healthcare planning is no longer theoretical. You've just seen the real-world difference between someone who restructures their plan with foresight — and someone who doesn't. These examples are here to help you visualize how a layered healthcare access plan can be built, and to prompt reflection on where your current approach may need to evolve. Because the goal here isn't just better care, it's access that's fully aligned with your lifestyle. And that starts with a plan designed around you.

If you're wondering where you stand today, ask yourself whether you know how long you'd wait for advanced imaging if symptoms appeared tomorrow. Consider whether your income would truly be protected if illness forced you to miss work. Think about whether your family could access care without relying entirely on employer benefits, and whether you have a trusted resource for second opinions, navigation, or international options. Finally, ask yourself if you could easily connect with specialists beyond the public system if the need arose.

These questions aren't meant to create fear — they're meant to reveal blind spots. Because the truth is, most people stop planning the moment they feel personally protected. They tick the box, assume they're covered, and move on. But the real test of a strong strategy is how well it holds up under pressure — not just for you, but for the people who depend on you.

Whether it's a spouse, a child, a parent, or even a business partner, your plan needs to reach beyond your own needs. It must account for shared risk, shifting responsibilities, and the ripple effect of illness on the people closest to you.

That's where we go next. Let's explore how to extend your strategy to protect those around you — and why that's the next essential step toward true resilience.

Extending the Strategy: Planning Beyond Yourself

The six steps you've just walked through are essential — but they only form the foundation of your plan. To be truly complete, your healthcare access strategy must extend beyond you. It needs to include the people who depend on you: your partner, children, and aging parents.

Most people don't realize the risk until it's too late. A spouse is diagnosed, and you become a caregiver overnight. Your child waits 12 to 18 months for an assessment that could've opened the door to early intervention. A parent's health suddenly declines, and you're pulled into a maze of decisions, expenses, and coordination — often while balancing work and your own wellbeing.

These aren't isolated examples. They're common scenarios. And they create ripple effects across your income, time, emotional energy, and long-term financial stability.

Spouses and Shared Risk

When a partner is affected by healthcare delays, the other often bears the brunt — emotionally, financially, and practically. You might be taking over and coordinating appointments, covering extra responsibilities at home, or even reducing work hours to provide care.

And yet, many plans are structured around just one individual. The corporate benefit plan may appear comprehensive, but these products never include anything other than health and dental for the other half, leaving gaps. Without careful review, couples can unknowingly fail to build plans that protect both of them against unexpected illness and accident.

Children and Delayed Access

While Canada's public healthcare system offers solid emergency care for children, it often fails when the concern is developmental, behavioral, or psychological. Diagnoses like autism or ADHD can come with 12–24 month waitlists. Mental health referrals may be denied for not being severe enough. And during that time, critical developmental windows close.

Planning for children means more than adding them to a benefits plan. It requires anticipating delays if the need arises, identifying private options for assessment and therapy, and ensuring your health spending account or insurance can cover the cost of timely intervention.

For families of children with chronic or lifelong conditions, the horizon extends far beyond high school, so you need to consider a plan that can also support long-term access planning to account for adulthood, independence, and ongoing care.

Aging Parents and Caregiver Strain

As parents age, their care needs can become increasingly complex — spanning medical, emotional, and financial challenges. When a health crisis strikes, it's often adult children who shoulder the burden: managing appointments, making tough decisions, and absorbing the emotional and logistical load. The stress can take a real toll, impacting your health, finances, and ability to work.

Yet few families plan for this in advance. Instead, they scramble — sometimes leading to conflict, burnout, or poor outcomes. Proactive planning means thinking through roles and responsibilities ahead of time, reviewing any existing coverage your parents may have, and preparing for the transitions and costs that may come.

When someone you love is denied timely care, the consequences affect you too — personally and professionally. That's why these conversations need to happen before you're in crisis mode, while you can still make decisions from a place of clarity, not urgency.

Pulling It All Together

At this point, your healthcare access strategy is no longer a single decision — it's a coordinated structure that must reflect not just your own needs, but the realities of those who rely on you. Your plan should now begin to account for how quickly you want access to care and what risks you're unwilling to take, along with your financial capacity and how much flexibility you have to fund care efficiently.

It should address gaps across both public and private healthcare layers and consider tax efficient funding models such as business structures, health spending accounts, or benefit plans where appropriate. It also needs to include support for your family — whether that means a spouse, children, or aging parents — and be designed with continuity and adaptability in mind, so it can evolve as your income, health, or life circumstances change.

It's a lot to manage — which is why many choose to work with someone who can help bring all these moving parts into alignment.

A New Kind of Specialist

We've mentioned the Certified Healthcare Access Planner™ (CHAP™) a few times throughout this chapter, so it makes sense to offer a bit more clarity here — especially if you're considering getting support from a specialist as you build or restructure your plan.

The CHAP™ designation is offered by the Institute of Certified Healthcare Access Planners™ (ICHAP™), an innovative organization focused on bridging the gap between healthcare and access. Through advisor education, their mission is to expand the scope of traditional risk planning.

CHAP™ professionals take a top-down, holistic approach. They're trained to assess healthcare access as a vital, standalone risk — one shaped by policy, politics, ideology, geography, awareness, waitlists, system strain, and gaps in both public and private care. From that perspective, they help clients build layered, adaptable insurance strategies that respond to both modern and traditional risks. They understand where the public system falls short, how international and private solutions can be integrated, and how to position plans to work even when the system doesn't.

This matters now more than ever. Canadian healthcare can no longer reliably deliver timely care — and the only way forward is to educate clients on the access risk, the urgency of proactive planning, and the expanding range of private options available. Earlier planning models didn't consider healthcare delays to be a threat, because they didn't have to. But that's no longer the case. What once seemed like a fringe concern is now central to how well your strategy performs when it matters most.

Whether you choose to implement your plan independently, or work with someone trained in this new method, you now have the insight to ask better questions, evaluate different solutions, and avoid outdated assumptions. But if you're looking for expert support, this is definitely the kind of planner you want in your corner — someone who understands both insurance risk management and the healthcare reality Canadians are navigating today.

Access isn't a guarantee. But with the right strategy, it can be a choice.

Completing the Structure

By now, you've seen what it takes to build a truly proactive healthcare access plan — one that protects not just your income, but your time, your mobility, your options, and your peace of mind. It's not just about insuring against illness — it's about building a system around yourself that works when you need it most.

This isn't easy work. It's strategic work. And as you've learned, the modern approach requires more than isolated products or blanket coverage. It demands clarity about your goals, an honest look at your risks, and the willingness to plan for the unexpected while there's still time to act.

Whether you build this structure on your own, or alongside a CHAP™ professional, what matters is that you're no longer depending on hope — you're working from a plan.

In the final chapter, we'll zoom out from the personal to the national. Because after everything we've covered, the question now becomes: If Canadians have to go to such lengths just to protect themselves, isn't it time we rethink the system itself?

The answer may lie in models we've yet to fully embrace — systems where public and private care don't compete but work in tandem, where innovation is welcomed, and where access isn't just a promise on paper, but a reality supported by smart policy and strategic design.

Chapter 11

Is it Possible There's a Better Model?

If Canadians need this much strategy, education, and insurance just to access timely care — we have to ask the bigger question:

Why is the system built this way in the first place?

Answering that means stepping back to examine how Canada's healthcare structure evolved — and the long running debate that has shaped it: privatization. For decades, the issue has repeatedly surfaced in policy discussions, typically in response to delays, funding shortfalls, or calls for reform. Most proposals haven't sought to dismantle the public system, but to relieve pressure, improve access, and introduce choice — all while preserving its core principles.

Still, the fear persists: that allowing private delivery of core services could weaken universality, deepen inequality, or pull resources from the public sector. These concerns deserve real attention — but so do the facts.

Around the world, countries facing the same challenges have taken a different approach. They've created hybrid systems that use public funding and private delivery together — not to compete, but to collaborate. And in many cases, those systems are delivering faster, more efficient, and more equitable care than Canada's.

This chapter isn't about promoting one model over another. It's about stepping back, setting aside ideology, and asking a practical question:

Are we using all the tools available — or just the ones we're politically comfortable with?

Let's start by examining the current reality in Canada — and then explore what's working elsewhere in comparison.

Canada's Reality: Outdated Framework, Growing Strain

Right now, Canada's healthcare model is difficult to define. To the casual observer, it still appears to be a purely one-tier, universal system. But for those who look closer, the picture is more complex: an overburdened public core funded by government, operating alongside a growing, unregulated private sector paid for directly by individuals. In practice, this creates an informal two-tier reality — one that is evolving rapidly.

Physicians Leaving the Public System

This shift is visible in many ways — and one of the clearest is the gradual exodus of physicians from public practice. In provinces like Quebec, British Columbia, and Alberta, a small but growing number of doctors have formally opted out of provincial billing to open fully private practices.

Their reasons are consistent: the bureaucracy that limits clinical autonomy, relentless patient volumes and administrative demands that fuel burnout, compensation models that fail to account for complex cases, and the inability to innovate under rigid system rules.

While these physicians represent only a fraction of the total workforce, their departure has ripple effects — shrinking public capacity, lengthening waitlists, and forcing patients who wish to follow their provider to pay out of pocket.

The Unacknowledged Two-Tier System

Despite this shift on the ground, government has largely avoided acknowledging the reality of a two-tier system.

Without coordinated regulation, promotion, or integration, the private side remains fragmented, with quality and accountability dependent on individual providers and contracts rather than a unified standard.

The question is no longer whether a two-tier system exists — it does. The real question is when and how policymakers will respond: Will they ignore it? Or will they regulate it intelligently, integrate it strategically, and ensure it improves access for more Canadians, not fewer?

Public Care, Private Delivery

On the surface, the system looks unchanged — your provincial health card still covers the cost. But behind the scenes, delivery is shifting. Increasingly, services like diagnostic imaging, outpatient surgeries, mental health care, and even oncology treatments are being performed outside public hospitals in privately owned clinics.

This hybrid model is expanding rapidly. In some cases, private delivery funded by the province reduces wait times and relieves pressure on public facilities. But it can also create uneven oversight, regional disparities, and limited transparency around how public dollars are spent.

These changes raise important questions: What happens if your province doesn't contract out the service you need? How do you know whether your provider is public, private, or both? And who ensures quality and accountability when care is outsourced?

The Quiet Decentralization of Healthcare

These shifts in delivery aren't the result of sweeping reforms or headline grabbing legislation. They're emerging through incremental contracts, regional pilot programs, and gradual structural changes — a quiet decentralization of Canadian healthcare in which access and quality increasingly depend on provincial policy, negotiated contracts, and local infrastructure. In practice, that often means the fastest or most flexible options are available only to those who can pay for them.

For those who want control over their care, the message is clear: the old model won't carry you forward. A strategic, informed approach is no longer optional — it's essential.

The Rise of Private Innovation

While the shift to private delivery is changing where care happens, emerging technology is transforming how it happens. A wave of healthcare innovators — entrepreneurs, technologists, and investors, many from outside traditional medicine — are reframing system inefficiencies as opportunities.

Across Canada, we're seeing AI-powered diagnostics, predictive health analytics, integrated wellness ecosystems, new insurance products, and subscription based access to care. These solutions are designed to deliver faster, more personalized outcomes, driven not by government policy but by patient demand, provider dissatisfaction, and private capital.

This isn't a theoretical future — it's already unfolding in clinics, startups, and digital platforms. The momentum of private innovation shows that change doesn't have to wait for government reform; it can come from targeted, creative solutions that address gaps in real time. But innovation on its own is not a complete solution.

For these changes to deliver lasting, equitable improvements, they need to be woven into a broader framework that protects universality, ensures quality, and expands access for everyone — not just those who can pay.

We've now examined how Canada's evolving hybrid model is taking shape — its strengths, weaknesses, and growing points of tension. The next step is to look outward: at countries that have successfully built balanced healthcare systems, where public and private sectors work together by design rather than by accident.

What Balanced Models Look Like

A truly balanced healthcare model doesn't ask the public and private sectors to compete — it asks them to complement each other. It's a deliberate design that uses public funding to protect universal access while leveraging private delivery to improve speed, choice, and innovation.

The goal isn't to replace the public system, but to strengthen it — reducing wait times, expanding capacity, and ensuring patients can access the right care, in the right place, at the right time. Around the world, some of the most respected healthcare systems have struck this balance, avoiding the weaknesses of fully public or fully private models. They show what's possible when private involvement is guided by public values — not driven solely by profit — and offer a blueprint for how Canada's system could evolve without compromising equity, compassion, or the foundational principles of universal care.

To see what this balance looks like in practice, let's look at countries that have built intentional partnerships between public and private care — starting with Germany's dual system.

Germany: A Dual System That Shares the Load

Germany is often cited as one of the most efficient and equitable healthcare systems in the world — and for good reason. It operates a well structured dual system that guarantees universal coverage while using private insurance to reduce strain on the public system and ensure higher earners contribute more.

Germany's healthcare system offers a clear example of how public and private insurance can work together effectively. Approximately 85% of the population is enrolled in statutory public health insurance, or *Gesetzliche Krankenversicherung* (GKV). This system is funded through income based contributions shared by both employees and employers and covers a wide range of services, including hospital care, physician visits, and prescription medications.

Those who earn above a certain annual income threshold — about €69,300 in 2024 — are required to leave the public plan and purchase private insurance, known as *Private Krankenversicherung* (PKV).

This dual structure serves two important purposes. First, it ensures that higher-income individuals contribute more directly to their own care, reducing pressure on the publicly funded system. Second, it helps balance demand by preventing heavy users with the means to pay from overwhelming public resources, promoting more efficient distribution and long term sustainability.

Private insurers in Germany compete for members, which encourages efficiency, responsiveness, and innovation.

Privately insured patients often benefit from shorter wait times, greater provider choice, and enhanced services — but they pay more for that access. Their premiums are also risk based, unlike the income based public model.

Efficiency, Access, and Fairness

Meanwhile, the public system continues to deliver high standards of care and ensures broad access across both urban and rural regions. It benefits from integrated electronic health records and administrative efficiency, helping to streamline services. Care remains free or low cost for the unemployed, elderly, and low-income residents, and wait times are generally reasonable.

What makes this system effective is its regulation. Both tiers are tightly governed to ensure transparency, fairness, and coordination. Physicians and hospitals serve patients in both systems, maintaining professional parity and continuity of care. There's no stigma around which plan you're in — because the structure isn't based on status, but on function and contribution.

Germany's model shows that dual systems don't have to create inequality. When built with the right safeguards, they can create balance: those who need public support receive it, those who can afford to pay more do so, and everyone benefits from reduced bottlenecks, timely access, and a more sustainable healthcare system. This isn't privatization. It's strategy — and it's a model Canada can learn from.

Where Germany uses income thresholds to balance demand and funding, France takes a different approach — regulating prices to preserve equity while allowing private enhancements.

France: Public Access With Private Enhancements

France consistently ranks among the top healthcare systems in the world — and much of that success comes from its ability to combine universal public access with carefully regulated private enhancements. The foundation of the system is strong: all residents are covered by public insurance funded through payroll and income taxes, providing comprehensive care that includes physician services, hospital stays, and prescriptions.

But what makes France's system distinctive is how it offers personalization without sacrificing equity. Many citizens choose to purchase complementary private insurance, known as *mutuelles,* to cover remaining out-of-pocket costs — such as co-payments, upgraded hospital rooms, faster access to specialists, and treatments not fully covered by the public plan. These enhancements give patients choice and speed, but public access remains guaranteed for all.

Affordability Is Built into the System

What sets France apart is how carefully it regulates pricing, ensuring that private participation doesn't lead to financial exclusion. The government sets maximum allowable fees for most services, keeping prices consistent and accessible—even when care is delivered by private providers.

Physicians who charge above standard rates are required to clearly disclose their fees, and even then, many of those additional costs are partially reimbursed by insurance. This regulatory structure helps prevent the kind of profit driven pricing that often undermines access in less controlled systems.

The result? Despite having both public and private care options, the average French citizen pays less out-of-pocket than their counterparts in many other developed countries. Patients enjoy minimal wait times, high efficiency, and broad choice — without sacrificing affordability or access.

A Model of Balance, Not Privilege

France proves that private care doesn't have to be expensive or elitist. When designed thoughtfully and regulated tightly, it can act as an enhancement layer — relieving pressure on the public system, improving the patient experience, and offering flexibility to those who want or need more.

And because the public system is robust, no one is left behind. Everyone has access. But those who want speed, upgrades, or customization can get it — affordably and transparently. This isn't privatization by stealth. It's policy over politics — and another example of how Canada could design private options without undermining its public values.

Like Germany, France proves that universal access and patient choice are not mutually exclusive — they simply require smart design.

Australia builds on this idea of balance but uses a different lever — tax incentives and policy tools — to actively manage participation in both public and private systems.

Australia: Designing Integration by Intent

Australia offers one of the clearest examples of how public and private healthcare can be intentionally blended — not just tolerated side by side but designed to complement each other. It's a system where universal access, market competition, and patient choice are built into the structure from the ground up.

Much of this innovation can be traced back to Medibank, a public health insurer launched in 1975. Initially created to compete with private insurers while supporting the goals of the public system, Medibank later evolved into a government owned enterprise — and eventually, a fully privatized company. But its influence endures: a healthcare landscape where public funding, private delivery, and consumer choice are integrated by design.

How the System Works Today

Australia's public health insurance system, Medicare, covers all citizens and permanent residents for treatment in public hospitals, general practitioner visits, and many specialist services. At the same time, citizens are strongly encouraged to purchase private insurance, which provides access to private hospitals, a choice of doctor, and faster elective procedures.

The government actively supports this dual approach by offering tax incentives for purchasing private insurance and imposing penalties—such as the Medicare Levy Surcharge—on high income earners who rely solely on public care.

A Strategic Division of Responsibility

What sets Australia's system apart is that it's not just passive coexistence between public and private care—it's an intentional load balancing mechanism. The public system ensures that no one is left without essential care, while the private sector absorbs demand from those seeking faster access or more personalized options, thereby relieving pressure on public infrastructure.

Additionally, the creation of Medibank, a government owned private insurer, helped normalize private competition within a public framework, proving that private enterprise can align with public goals when guided by clear policy.

Access, Satisfaction, and Equity

The results are clear. Wait times in Australia are significantly lower than in Canada, patient satisfaction is high, and access isn't determined by wealth — but by the system's ability to offer options within a regulated framework.

Australia's model shows that governments don't have to fear private enterprise. When used strategically, it strengthens public systems rather than weakens them. It's not about creating winners and losers — it's about building resilience. This is how policy and profit can work together — not at the expense of equity, but in support of it.

Switzerland offers yet another variation, demonstrating how even a fully private insurance framework can deliver universal access when regulation is precise and equity is built into the design.

Switzerland: Private Insurance With Universal Access

Switzerland offers one of the most compelling counterarguments to the idea that private healthcare inevitably undermines equity. In fact, it demonstrates the opposite: that private insurance can deliver universal access—when designed with intention and regulated rigorously.

Every resident of Switzerland is legally required to purchase health insurance from a private provider. But this is far from a free-market free-for-all. It's a tightly structured system in which all insurers must offer standardized benefit packages that include a comprehensive set of essential services. Prices for these services are regulated, and insurers are prohibited from making a profit on basic health coverage. To ensure affordability, income-based subsidies are provided to help lower-income individuals and families cover their premiums.

This approach creates a marketplace with real consumer choice, but without sacrificing access or fairness.

Competition Within a Framework of Equity

Despite being delivered through private insurers, Switzerland's healthcare system remains transparent, accountable, and efficient. Patients know exactly what's covered and what it costs. Insurers are held to strict quality standards and performance benchmarks. Competition encourages high service quality and innovation, but never at the expense of essential coverage.

All citizens are covered. All have access. While individuals can choose to pay more for upgrades or supplementary services, the essentials are guaranteed—for everyone.

Together, these countries prove that the issue isn't whether private care exists — it's how it's designed and regulated. Their experiences offer valuable lessons for Canada as it considers how to modernize healthcare while preserving its core principles

Learning From the World, Not Fearing It

International models show us that private care doesn't have to mean privatization. In fact, when carefully designed and rigorously regulated, private participation can reinforce public values—rather than erode them. Countries like Germany, France, Australia, and Switzerland blend public oversight with private delivery to create systems that are both inclusive and efficient.

These systems benefit from the innovation and responsiveness often found in the private sector, while maintaining universal access through clear regulations, income-based protections, and standardized coverage. Private providers help reduce wait times, expand patient choice, and ease the burden on government-run facilities—without sacrificing equity.

While the idea of stratified access often raises concern, these examples show that it isn't inherently unfair. What matters is how options are structured and communicated, and whether strong oversight ensures that the baseline level of care remains high and accessible to all.

The lesson for Canada is clear: there is no need to fear private options, as long as they're built intentionally. With the right policies, incentives, and regulatory guardrails, private care can complement and strengthen the public system—improving the healthcare experience for everyone, not just a privileged few.

The Real Issue Isn't Private Care – It's Policy Design

Critics often argue that integrating private care into core service delivery threatens universality and equity. But real world experience suggests the opposite: when guided by clear principles and sound policy, private involvement can actually protect and enhance these values.

In countries that have adopted balanced models, private options don't siphon resources from the public system — they relieve it. By offering faster access to elective or non-urgent care, private providers allow public resources to be focused where they're most needed: on vulnerable populations and time sensitive treatment. This targeted approach improves efficiency and fairness across the system.

The fear of a two-tier system also rests on a false assumption — that any private choice automatically creates inequality. But in countries like France and Germany, private care operates within national frameworks that regulate pricing, ensure transparency, and prohibit exclusion. Choosing to pay more for upgrades doesn't come at someone else's expense, because the baseline level of care remains strong, universal, and equitable.

One of the most persistent misconceptions in Canada is that any introduction of private healthcare will automatically lead us down the path of an American style system — one where access is based on income, not need. But this fear is rooted more in rhetoric than reality. Most developed countries with private options look nothing like the United States. Their systems are built on universal coverage, robust public oversight, and transparent regulation.

Private care exists, but it operates within frameworks that limit profit motives and prioritize access.

The United States, by contrast, has a fragmented, commercialized, and largely employer based healthcare system. There is no universal baseline of care, and out-of-pocket costs can be unpredictable and catastrophic. That outcome isn't inevitable when private care is involved — it's the result of poor design and the absence of regulatory guardrails. Countries like Germany, France, and Switzerland prove that when private involvement is guided by public values — and not left unchecked — it can coexist with fairness, access, and system wide sustainability.

Ultimately, it's not private participation that creates inequity — it's poorly designed policy. When integrated with intention and oversight, private care becomes a tool for system wide sustainability, not a threat to it.

The Practical Case for Private Planning

Across the world, balanced healthcare models have shown us that public and private care are not adversaries — they are potential partners. When private participation is regulated with precision, designed with intent, and grounded in public values, it can relieve pressure on the public system, expand patient choice, and protect universality.

The message for Canada is unmistakable: the real risk isn't in private care — it's in failing to design it well. Our current hybrid system is already here, but without a strategy, without consistent oversight, and without a plan to make it work for everyone. Left unmanaged, it will continue to grow in ways that deepen inequity and confusion. Managed well, it could become a cornerstone of sustainability and access.

Ultimately, the debate is not about whether private care should exist — it's about whether we are willing to use all the tools available to us, or only the ones we're politically comfortable with. That was the bigger question at the start of this chapter — and the answer will determine whether Canadians can access the care they need, when they need it, without being left behind.

Chapter 12

Strategy, Not Surrender

When I began writing this book, I thought about every client who's ever called me feeling shattered — needing healthcare they couldn't get, on a timeline they couldn't influence.

As a consultant, I see the same pattern over and over: people blindsided by delays and left with few, if any, options — frustrated, helpless, and financially unprepared for the unexpected. Many have payout strategies, but they're reactive, focused on coping with a crisis after it happens rather preventing one.

At the very start, I talked about a paradigm shift: moving from passive reliance on the public system to proactive, deliberate planning that includes private options. My hope is that by now, you not only understand what I meant — you recognize it as the only way forward.

This isn't just a change in thinking; it's the difference between being at the mercy of a waitlist and taking control of your healthcare outcomes.

It's tempting to look abroad at countries that have successfully blended public and private care with insurance to fund both. Those models can be inspiring — but they aren't our reality. This book was never about idealizing other systems. It was about helping you navigate the one we have.

After 45 years, our infrastructure hasn't kept pace with our population, our needs, or the medical technology available today. People are dying on waitlists. We cannot wait for policy to catch up. We need solutions now.

Some solutions already exist — and this is why it's imperative that Canadians understand exactly what we're dealing with: how the system works, how the private sector operates, and what healthcare insurance options are available right now. Because this is where our choices are today.

We can, and should, continue to hope that the public system will improve — that Canada will evolve, and that our government will work together to create a regulated, insured, and balanced model where public and private care co-exist without waitlists. But hope alone isn't a plan. It must run in the background while we build a culture of modern, proactive planning for the here and now.

Choosing private care doesn't mean abandoning public values or Canadian identity. It means protecting what matters most: your time, your livelihood, your family, and your ability to recover and contribute. Today, it's not a luxury — it's a necessity, because you may not be able to get the care you need when you need it. And for some, it can be the difference between life and death.

This is the moment to make the shift — from waiting and hoping to planning and acting. Because healthcare isn't about politics. It's about survival. And waiting isn't a strategy. Planning is.

The next move is yours.

It's time to get **Off the Waitlist.**

About the Author

Ingrid Gahsner is a licensed insurance professional with more than 30 years of experience spanning insurance, investments, and corporate benefit consulting. Through her firm, IMI Canada, she develops protection strategies that are healthcare access focused — helping clients safeguard their time, health, and financial security from the risk of delay.

Her innovative approach has resulted in a successful practice and established her as a recognized authority in insurance based planning, an emerging discipline that focuses on the intersection of healthcare and protection strategy. Ingrid is the main creator of the CHAP™ curriculum and serves on the Board of Directors of the Institute of Certified Healthcare Access Planners™ (ICHAP™), where she contributes to the advancement of professional education in this field.

Based in Toronto, she lives with her family and is an active advocate for smarter, more strategic healthcare solutions — including private insurance innovations and meaningful national policy reform. Her advocacy is driven by a clear goal: to reduce waitlists and eliminate the harmful delays that prevent Canadians from accessing timely medical care.

Visit www.imicanada.co to learn more, schedule a call, or book a consultation.

Consulting Services

The purpose of this book has been to illuminate the reality of Canada's healthcare system and to provide readers with a deeper understanding of the challenges it presents. My goal has been to equip you with the knowledge and confidence to make informed decisions about your own care, while also drawing attention to the alternatives that exist outside the public system.

If, having reached this point, you feel it's necessary to evaluate your own circumstances — to take a clear inventory of what you have — or don't have — you're not alone. Far too often, individuals assume they are adequately protected, only to discover, sometimes at great cost, that the system doesn't function as they believed. What feels sufficient today may prove inadequate tomorrow, and the price of inaction can be substantial when it comes to healthcare delay.

If you would like to review your current insurance port-folio, establish a plan that reflects the realities of today's healthcare landscape, or simple schedule a call to discuss the products / information provided in this book, I would be happy to oblige.

Please connect with me via email or through the website.

Ingrid Gahsner,

ingrid.gahsner@imicanada.co

www.imicanada.co

Because when it comes to your health, the right plan's not optional — **it's essential.**

Disclaimer

This book does not provide insurance, investment, planning or medical advice beyond the scope of applicable licensing and credentials. It introduces the concept of healthcare access planning — a new proactive discipline created by delays in the public healthcare system, and explores protection strategies from an insurance based perspective to safeguard against this liability.

Any planning information provided, explained, or recommended in this book is offered strictly within this context and should not be confused with holistic financial planning advice as provided by a Certified Financial Planner (CFP®). While there may be overlapping terminology within the financial services industry — and while I draw on decades of knowledge and experience across insurance, investments, and risk management — it's important to clarify that this book, and any recommendations within it, are aligned with my current credentials and licensing, which is limited to insurance and investment advice permitted under the LLQP.

In addition, for absolute clarity, I'm not referring, recommending, or providing direction with respect to any specific private healthcare providers, practitioners, or clinics. I am not a medical doctor, nor do I hold any certification or medical expertise. All healthcare related information in this book is presented as a result of general research and, to the best of my ability, has been reviewed and verified against credible third party medical sources to ensure accuracy.

Glossary of Terms

Glossary

Access Planning

A proactive approach to structuring your healthcare strategy, insurance, and financial resources to ensure faster, more reliable access to medical care when you need it most.

Actuarial

Relating to the work of actuaries, particularly the use of statistical and mathematical methods to evaluate financial risk in insurance, pensions, and healthcare planning. Actuarial data is used to set premiums, forecast claims, and design sustainable coverage models.

Benefit Limits

The maximum amount an insurance policy will pay for a particular service, treatment, or condition — either annually, per lifetime, or per claim.

Biologic

A high-cost medication derived from living cells, used to treat complex diseases like cancer or autoimmune disorders. Biologics often require special handling and approval processes.

Boutique Hospitals

Privately funded, full-service medical facilities that offer personalized care, shorter wait times, and access to advanced treatments. These hospitals often serve high-income individuals seeking premium medical services outside the public system.

Canada Health Act

The federal legislation that outlines the principles of publicly funded healthcare in Canada, including universality, accessibility, and portability. It restricts private billing for publicly insured services.

Canada Health Transfer (CHT)

The largest federal transfer payment to provinces and territories, providing funding for healthcare under the principles of the Canada Health Act. The CHT helps support public healthcare systems and is distributed on a per-capita basis, with some adjustments for tax points and equalization.

Catastrophic Coverage

Insurance that protects against large, unexpected health-care costs, often with high deductibles but broad coverage for serious medical events.

CHAP™ (Certified Healthcare Access Planner)

A certified professional trained to help individuals design, implement, and manage personalized healthcare access strategies using private, public, and global solutions.

Concierge Medicine

A private healthcare model in which patients pay a membership or retainer fee for enhanced access to their physician. Services often include same-day appointments, extended visits, 24/7 communication, and personalized care coordination outside the constraints of the public system.

Covered Illnesses

The specific conditions listed in a critical illness insurance policy. The policy only pays out if the insured is diagnosed with one of these defined illnesses.

Critical Illness Insurance

A type of coverage that pays a lump sum if the insured is diagnosed with a specified serious illness, such as cancer, heart attack, or stroke. Intended to offset lost income or unexpected costs during recovery.

Diagnostic Delays

The wait time before accessing necessary medical tests (like MRIs or CT scans) in the public system — often a major bottleneck in treatment timelines.

Disability Insurance

Coverage that replaces a portion of your income if you're unable to work due to illness or injury. Policies may differ based on definitions of disability and occupation class.

Drug Cap

The maximum amount an insurance plan will pay for prescription drugs in a year or over a lifetime. Once exceeded, the patient must pay out of pocket.

Exclusion

A specific condition, treatment, or circumstance that is not covered under an insurance policy. Exclusions limit the insurer's liability and are clearly outlined in the policy contract, often applying to pre-existing conditions, experimental treatments, or high-risk activities.

Extended Health Insurance

Additional private health coverage beyond what's publicly funded. Includes drug, dental, vision, paramedical, and sometimes private medical services.

Fee-for-Service Care

Private medical care where patients pay out of pocket for each service. Used to bypass delays or access services not covered publicly.

Functional Medicine

A personalized, systems-based approach to healthcare that focuses on identifying and addressing the root causes of disease. Functional medicine practitioners often use detailed patient histories, advanced diagnostics, and integrative treatments that may not be part of conventional care models.

Global Healthcare Access

Strategic planning that includes the option to receive medical care outside Canada, often to reduce wait times or access unavailable treatments.

Guaranteed Issue Policy

An insurance policy available without medical underwriting. Typically includes limited benefits and higher premiums due to broader risk acceptance.

Healthcare Access Planning

A strategic process that evaluates and structures an individual's public, private, and global healthcare options to reduce wait times, improve care outcomes, and ensure timely access to services. It often includes insurance analysis, financial alignment, and provider coordination.

Health Spending Account (HSA)

A tax-advantaged account that allows business owners or employers to reimburse employees for eligible healthcare expenses. HSAs provide flexibility in covering medical, dental, and vision costs not covered by provincial plans or traditional insurance.

ICHAP™ (Institute for Certified Healthcare Access Planning)

An educational and certification body that trains and accredits professionals in healthcare access planning. ICHAP™ develops industry standards, provides ongoing training, and supports the growth of the Certified Healthcare Access Planner™ designation.

Insurance Companies Act

Federal legislation that governs the regulation, supervision, and operation of insurance companies in Canada. It outlines requirements for licensing, capital adequacy, financial reporting, and consumer protection, and is administered by the Office of the Superintendent of Financial Institutions (OSFI).

Integrative Medicine

A holistic approach to healthcare that combines conventional Western medicine with complementary therapies such as acupuncture, nutrition, chiropractic, and mindfulness. It emphasizes treating the whole person — body, mind, and spirit — with evidence-informed methods.

Medically Necessary

A service or treatment deemed essential for the diagnosis or treatment of a health condition, as defined by provincial health systems or insurers. Only these are typically covered publicly.

Medical Tourism

The practice of traveling to another country to receive medical treatment, often to access care more quickly, affordably, or at a level of specialization not available locally. Common procedures include surgeries, diagnostics, and advanced therapies.

Non-Invasive

Refers to medical procedures or tests that don't require breaking the skin or entering the body. Often seen as lower risk and faster to access.

Non-Surgical Hospital Facility

A medical facility that provides inpatient or outpatient care without performing surgical procedures. These facilities typically offer diagnostics, rehabilitation, chronic disease management, infusion therapy, or palliative care under medical supervision.

Nurse Practitioner (NP)

A highly trained registered nurse with advanced education and clinical experience, authorized to diagnose conditions, prescribe medications, and manage patient care independently. NPs often fill gaps in access to primary care, particularly in underserved or high-demand areas.

Pre-existing Condition

A medical condition that existed before applying for an insurance policy. It may affect eligibility, require exclusions, or result in modified coverage terms unless specifically disclosed and accepted by the insurer.

Primary Care

The first point of contact in the healthcare system for non-emergency issues. Typically provided by family doctors or general practitioners, primary care includes prevention, diagnosis, treatment, and coordination of specialist referrals.

Prior Authorization

A requirement from an insurer for pre-approval before certain tests, medications, or procedures are covered — often used for expensive or complex treatments.

Private Health Clinics

Clinics operating outside the public system that offer faster access to diagnostics, specialist consultations, and elective procedures for a direct fee.

Privatization

The shift of healthcare services from public funding and delivery to private pay or private insurance models. Often debated in Canadian policy.

Reinsurance

Insurance for insurance companies — used to spread the financial risk of very large or catastrophic claims, particularly in health or life insurance.

Self-Insuring

When an individual or organization chooses to pay for healthcare expenses out of pocket instead of using insurance. High-risk unless well-planned.

Specialty Drug

A high-cost prescription medication used to treat complex or rare conditions. Typically requires prior authorization and may exceed drug caps.

Stem Cell Therapy

A medical treatment that uses stem cells to repair or replace damaged tissues and organs. Often considered regenerative medicine, stem cell therapy is used in conditions like orthopedic injuries, autoimmune diseases, and certain cancers. Access may be limited or unavailable through the public system in Canada.

Stop-Loss Insurance

A form of catastrophic coverage that limits your total financial exposure by kicking in once medical costs pass a certain threshold.

Supplemental Plans

Private insurance policies designed to cover healthcare costs not included in government-funded plans. These may include prescription drugs, dental, vision, paramedical services, travel insurance, or enhanced access to private care and specialists.

Surgical Clinics

Privately operated medical facilities that perform elective or specialized surgical procedures outside the public hospital system. These clinics often reduce wait times and provide faster access to surgeries not considered urgent in the public system.

Survival Clause

A condition in critical illness insurance requiring the insured to survive a set number of days after diagnosis (often 30) for the benefit to be paid.

Telehealth

The delivery of healthcare services remotely using phone, video, or secure messaging platforms. Telehealth allows patients to consult with doctors, access follow-ups, and receive certain treatments without visiting a clinic or hospital in person.

Total Disability

A definition used in disability insurance that refers to a complete inability to perform the essential duties of one's occupation due to illness or injury.

www.ingramcontent.com/pod-product-compliance
Lightning Source LLC
Chambersburg PA
CBHW051245020426
42333CB00025B/3056